D1243883

An Encyclopedia of
Ribbon Embroidery
Holiday Designs

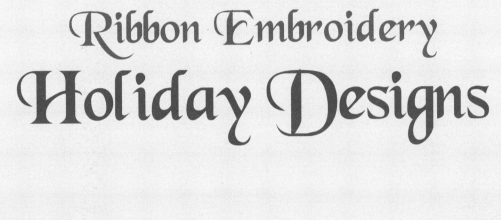

Bobbie Matela, Managing Editor
Carol Wilson Mansfield, Art Director
Jane Cannon Meyers, Creative Director
Ann Harnden, Editor
Pam Nichols and Carly Poggemeyer,
    Assistant Editors
Mary Hernandez, Book Design

Color plates and covers stitched by:
Susan Agonia, Linda Causee,
and Carol Levick.

If you enjoy ribbon embroidery, look for these other American School of Needlework® books where this book was purchased, or write to the publisher.

Learn to do Ribbon Embroidery in Just One Day (ASN 3404)
An Encyclopedia of Ribbon Embroidery Flowers (ASN 3405)
Ribbon Embroidery Alphabets (ASN 3406)
101 Iron-On Transfers for Ribbon Embroidery (ASN 3407)
An Encyclopedia of Ribbon Embroidery Birds, Butterflies, and Blossoms (ASN 3408)
An Encyclopedia of Ribbon Embroidery Fruits, Vegetables, and Herbs (ASN 3409)

For a full-color catalog including books of cross stitch designs, write to:

**American School of Needlework®, Consumer Division
1455 Linda Vista Drive, San Marcos, CA 92069**

*We have made every effort to ensure the accuracy and completeness of these instructions.
We cannot, however, be responsible for human error, typographical mistakes, or variations in individual work.*

©1997 by Kooler Design Studio, Inc.
Published by American School of Needlework®, Inc.; ASN Publishing, 1455 Linda Vista Drive, San Marcos, CA 92069

ISBN: 0-88195-825-5   All rights reserved.   Printed in U.S.A.   1 2 3 4 5 6 7 8 9

Introduction

As needleworkers, we love to memorialize special days with our personal handiwork. This wonderful collection of 145 ribbon embroidery designs will provide you with ideas to stitch throughout the years.

If you haven't tried stitching with ribbon before, there are a few special techniques to learn—see pages 4 to 13. Once you've read through the background information at the beginning of this book you'll be ready to choose any of the motifs photographed on pages 17 to 20 or the covers. Then find the stitching guide in the back of the book—pages 22 to 60. These guides are the blueprints for creating your own beautiful ribbonwork. It helps to refer to the photographs when stitching, but if your ribbon stitches don't look exactly like the photographed ribbon, there's no need to be concerned. Each time a stitcher picks up needle and ribbon, it tends to look slightly different. But the results are always beautiful!

The talented designer of these motifs, Deanna Hall West, is a self-confessed sentimentalist. She has many fond memories of family holiday traditions. Her mother taught her basic stitching and sewing skills and instilled in her a deep love and appreciation for all things hand-stitched. Deanna dedicates this book to her mother and to her supportive sons, Christopher and Jeffrey—who are the celebrations of her life!

Contents

Ribbon Embroidery Basics

Supplies

Ribbon

Ribbons used for embroidery are chosen for their special properties. They must drape nicely and be able to be pulled through fabric without damage to the ribbon or the fabric. Silk and the recently manufactured silk substitutes (silky polyester and rayon) can be used for embroidery.

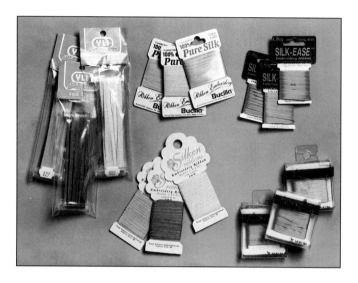

For ribbon embroidery, 4mm is the most commonly used width. Some companies produce many individual colors, while other brands specialize in variegated ribbons—where color values change along the length of a single ribbon. In addition to 4mm, many of our designs use 7mm ribbon, although the color range of 7mm is more limited than that of 4mm. You may also be able to find some wider, 13mm ribbon. If so, you can use it effectively any time a design calls for two or more adjacent stitches of 7mm ribbon (e.g., Chocolates on page 22).

Mixing ribbon widths adds to the textural contrast which is a strong aspect of this embroidery. For a delightful change of pace, the new sheer organza ribbons can also be used (e.g., Pink Candy on page 45.)

The stitching guides on pages 22-60 list the colors to be used for each of the designs. Refer to the Ribbon Color Conversion Key on pages 14-15 for suggestions when substituting different brands of ribbon.

Work with ribbon cut into 10"-12" (or shorter) pieces. Embroidery ribbons are relatively fragile, and during the stitching process the ribbon can be easily frayed. Short lengths help to prevent any damage.

Threads

Cotton embroidery floss is often used with ribbon to create narrow lines of embroidery, tack down a portion of a stitch, or to preserve a special shape. When floss is required for construction of a motif, we have listed a generic color name for the floss, usually to match the ribbon with which it is used. You can also use any of the following embroidery threads with great success:

Rayon, six-strand floss
Silk, six- or seven-strand floss
Crewel yarn, very fine wool
Floche, five-ply cotton
Flower thread, twisted matte-finish cotton
Marlitt, or similar-weight rayon thread
Pearl cotton, size 12 or 8

Needles

Basically, three types of needles are used for ribbon embroidery. We find that all kinds have their place. You can choose a sharp chenille needle or a blunt tapestry needle for ribbon stitching, and a crewel needle for fine threads.

One important factor to consider when choosing the correct needle is the size of the eye. With silk ribbon the needle's eye should be large enough for the ribbon to pass through easily, with little or no gathering. Also, the size of the needle's shaft needs to be large enough that a sufficient hole is made in the background fabric to accommodate the ribbon as it passes through the fabric without causing too much friction, which can further damage the ribbon. In sizing, the higher the number, the smaller the needle.

A chenille needle is a large sharp needle with a large eye. Size 18 chenille is used for most embroidery with 4mm- and 7mm-wide ribbon.

A tapestry needle, with a blunt tip, of a size equivalent to the sharp chenille needle can also be used any time you want to be sure not to pierce the threads of the background fabric or any of the stitching ribbon.

An embroidery or crewel needle is a fine sharp needle with a large eye. This needle style is appropriate when embellishing a ribbon design with floss, silk thread, or any of the other accessory threads. The needle size will depend on the thread size and the number of strands used.

Fabrics

Any fabric with a medium weave will work as a background fabric. Knitted fabrics are often too loose to hold ribbon embroidery securely, but can be used if a lightweight non-stretch backing fabric is attached.

Some fabric suggestions are:
Dressmaking fabrics—cotton, voile, silk, batiste, faille, moiré
Evenweave embroidery fabrics—plain weaves like linen, cottage cloth, Jobelan®, Lugana, or complex weaves like Aida and hardanger
Linen twill—often used for crewel embroidery
Specially-packaged ribbon embroidery fabric

For ribbon-embellished clothing, choose a fabric that does not require much ironing. A lightweight interfacing can be attached to the back of the fabric to prevent puckering around the embroidery. The garment needs to be laundered according to the ribbon manufacturer's washing instructions.

The back of ribbon embroidery is certainly not neat! If you are working on a ready-made garment, you might wish to remove enough of the lining to do your stitching, then replace the lining to cover the back of your work. If there is no lining, consider attaching a soft material to the wrong side of the stitched area.

Scissors

Small, sharp embroidery scissors are needed. Besides cutting the ribbon and embroidery threads, the flat surface of the blade used in a stroking manner can help to spread the ribbon where it emerges from the fabric.

Frames and Hoops

The best ribbon embroidery results are achieved when the background fabric is held under tension during the stitching process. Use an appropriately sized embroidery hoop, especially when working on clothing, or needlework stretcher bars. If the previously worked stitching needs to be held in place while constructing the adjacent stitching, you will need a small hoop so you can hold with one hand and stitch with the other.

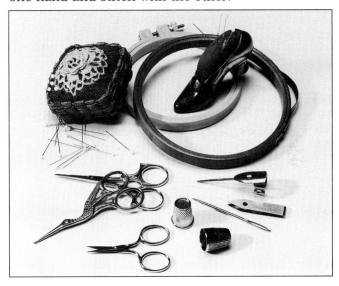

Additional Handy Tools

The following tools and supplies are helpful in creating a beautifully finished project:

Water-soluble marking pens or transfer pencils—to transfer a design to a light background fabric; use a light pen or pencil for dark fabrics.

Water-soluble fabric stabilizer—on which a design is traced, attacted to background fabric, and later removed with water.

Trolley needle—to manipulate, spread, and adjust the ribbon.

Cotton swab (lightly moistened)—to remove any water-soluble marks on the fabric that are not covered by your embroidery.

Stilletto, awl or large-diameter needle—to puncture holes into tightly woven fabric, preventing wide ribbon from being damaged.

A soft handkerchief or facial tissue—to cover stitching that might be distorted by a hoop.

Small crochet hook—to tidy up back of work.

Special Techniques

Marking a Design on Fabric

You may work any motif in a free-form manner, or you may draw a design outline directly on the background fabric. Place fabric directly over the design and trace with a water-soluble fabric-marking pen. If the fabric is heavy, a lightbox will be helpful. You can also use a #2 lead pencil (for light to medium-colored fabrics) or a white pencil (for dark fabrics).

Another transfer method is with the use of some tulle or other open mesh fabric. Trace the design onto the tulle, place the tulle over the background fabric and retrace the lines with pencil or removable pen; enough of the design should transfer through the holes of the tulle for reasonably accurate stitching.

You can also trace the design on water-soluble fabric stabilizer. Baste the stabilizer to the fabric, work embroidery, then remove basting threads and dissolve the stabilizer with a spray of water.

You may also work ribbon embroidery with just position marks on the fabric, rather than a full pattern. This approach works especially well for a stem or branch. Draw the basic stem lines, then locations for the intended leaves, and stitch accordingly.

Threading the Needle

Thread the end through eye, and pull it through beyond the tip of the needle. Pierce the ribbon end with the needle, **Fig 1**. Holding point of needle, pull the long end of the ribbon to secure it.

Fig 1

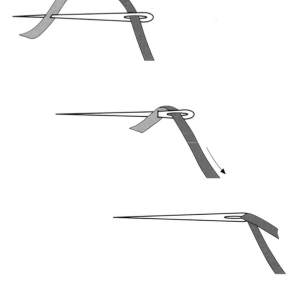

Making a Knot

To begin stitching, make this special knot, **Fig 2**, at end of ribbon. Drape ribbon end over needle; wrap working ribbon once around needle, then pull needle through the wrap to form a knot. When you begin to stitch, be careful not to pull too tightly, or the knot may come through the fabric.

Fig 2

Ending the Ribbon

When you finish using a color, run the needle under a few stitches on the wrong side, **Fig 3**. The ribbon should end, whenever possible, toward the center of the stitching area to avoid being visible beyond the edge of the embroidery. If desired, pierce through some ribbon on the back before cutting the end, but make sure this does not disturb the front of your work. For added security, use floss or thread to tack ends together on back of work.

Fig 3

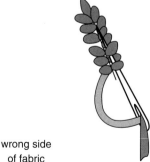

wrong side
of fabric

Stitching Tips

- Work with short ribbon lengths (10"-12") to prevent excessive ribbon damage.

- To remove wrinkles and folds in silk ribbon, gently pull the ribbon over a moistened piece of synthetic sponge. While ribbon is still moist, pull it between your thumb and forefinger, then let dry on a flat surface. Synthetic or silk ribbon can also be flattened using a warm iron.

- If you do not find a ribbon color in the right size, you can use a wider ribbon and pull it tightly; two smaller widths of ribbon can also be used in place of a larger size.

- Keep ribbon untwisted on back of fabric; this makes it easier to spread out the stitches on the front of the fabric. If your ribbon comes up through the fabric looking twisty, turn to the wrong side and straighten the ribbon as needed.

- Use thumb (or thumbnail) and forefinger of your non-stitching hand to hold previously worked stitches in place while working the next adjacent stitch. This helps prevent previous stitches from being pulled too tightly or even being rearranged into a visual disaster.

- Don't carry your ribbon from one area to the next as you stitch. Not only will it possibly show through on the front, but as you stitch other colors in those areas, the carried ribbon will get in the way.

- Avoid stitching through ribbon and knots on back of fabric. Nudge needle tip around ribbon on the back to find an open stitching location. If your stitching ribbon is pulled through an already-worked stitch, it can cause distortion or damage to the existing stitch.

- You may be working with two (or more) threaded needles (perhaps one with silk ribbon and the other with floss) at the same time. To prevent a tangled mess and pulled stitches, bring the idle needle temporarily to rest on the front of the fabric, parking it away from the working area. You can also hold excess ribbon out of the way with a long silk straight pin.

- If a section of ribbon will not stay where it is supposed to, use matching floss to tack it in place. To tidy up the wrong side, use a small crochet hook to pull ribbon ends beneath stitches.

- To remove anchored ribbon from the needle's eye, gently pull on the short pierced end to loosen the knot, then pull ribbon off needle.

Using the Designs

These motifs have been designed using 4mm and 7mm ribbons. The stitched examples on the covers and color pages 17-20 are shown actual size.

Refer to the covers and color pages to choose the motif(s) you want to stitch. The Stitching Guides for each of the fourteen Holiday categories are given on pages 22-60. Follow the stitching sequence, and refer to the labels which show ribbon color and size and the stitch to use. The Stitching Guides are the same size as the stitched samples, so you can match the size as you work.

You can enlarge or reduce any of the motifs as long as you remember the limitations of the ribbon width. To enlarge, you can add more stitches or change to a wider ribbon, whichever looks best. For some of the wide motifs you can work one 13mm ribbon stitch instead of two 7mm stitches.

To reduce, you can use a narrower ribbon or take smaller (or fewer) stitches and/or pull the stitches more tightly. Always test-stitch a prototype of the new size on scrap fabric before incorporating it into your design.

Ribbon embroidery is a technique that allows quite a bit of freedom with scale. It is perfectly fine to have an apple that is as large as a balloon. Of greater importance is the visual effect; it should be pleasing to the eye rather than a realistic size. And if you wish to work with different colors than we have chosen, feel free to do so.

Finishing Considerations

If your piece was worked on a frame, there will probably be no blocking required. If the finished embroidery is to be washed, pre-test the ribbon to make sure it is colorfast. Dip a small piece in water and place on a paper towel; let dry and check to see if the dye runs. If the ribbon is not colorfast, but the item must be washed, choose another ribbon. If you must wash, use cold water with mild soap and a cold water rinse.

When working on a ready-made garment, take into account the surface fabric needs as well as the embroidery. If you must take an iron to it, press face down on a thick padded surface—a terry cotton towel is an excellent choice—only lightly pressing the areas of stitching. Use caution to prevent scorching.

When framing, you may wish to protect the embroidery with glass. Because of the textural quality, choose a shadow box frame or insert spacers to keep the glass from touching the stitches.

Ribbon Embroidery Stitches

The stitch diagrams are shown using ribbon. When stitching with embroidery floss, use the same method and, unless otherwise directed, use two strands of floss.

When working any stitch, bring ribbon (or floss) up from back to front of fabric at odd (1, 3, 5) numbers and stitch down through fabric at even (2, 4, 6) numbers unless otherwise directed. Secondary stitching is labelled with sequential letters (A, B, C, etc.)

The stitches and their variations are in the following alphabetical order:

Backstitches (2)
Colonial Knot
Couching
Fly Stitch
French Knot
Gathering Stitch
Lazy Daisy Stitches (3)
Loop Stitch
Ribbon Stitches (6)
Spider Web
Stem Stitch
Straight Stitches (6)
Tack Stitch
Weaving
Wrapped Bar

Backstitches

The basic Backstitch is followed by one variation.

Backstitch

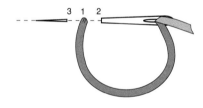

Bring needle up at 1, a stitch length away from beginning of design line. Stitch back down at 2, at beginning of line. Bring needle up at 3, then stitch back down to meet previous stitch (same hole as 1). Continue, carrying ribbon forward beneath fabric and stitching backward on the surface to meet previous stitch. Backstitch can be worked along curving or straight lines.

Wrapped Backstitch

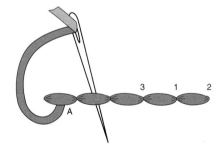

Work a row of Backstitch (above). Bring ribbon up at A, below last Backstitch and proceed to wrap each consecutive Backstitch once or twice by slipping needle beneath Backstitch, but not piercing the fabric. Stitch down into fabric to end.

Colonial Knot

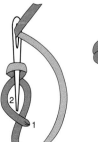

This makes a larger knot than the French Knot (page 9). Bring ribbon up at 1. Swing ribbon in a clockwise loop; follow arrow and slip point of needle beneath ribbon from left to right. Bring working ribbon around point of needle in a figure eight motion.

Insert needle at 2, near 1; needle will be vertical. Pull ribbon loosely around needle as you pull needle through to back of fabric. Do not pull too tightly.

Couching

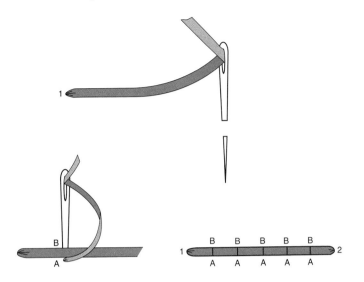

This technique requires one ribbon laid on the fabric and a second ribbon (or floss) to hold the first ribbon in place. Bring needle and ribbon up at 1, the left side of outline to be couched. Pull ribbon through, along intended couched position, and park it temporarily at right side of fabric.

Hold ribbon flat and bring second needle with ribbon (or floss) up at A, below flat ribbon. Stitch down above flat ribbon (B), making a vertical stitch. Proceed to next couching point and repeat. At end of row, pass flat ribbon needle through to back of fabric (2) and secure it.

Fly Stitch

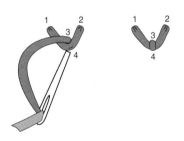

Bring needle up at 1 and insert at 2; flatten the ribbon as you pull partially through. Bring needle up at 3, making sure loop is beneath needle. Pull ribbon toward yourself to form a "V" and insert needle at 4 to hold in place.

French Knot

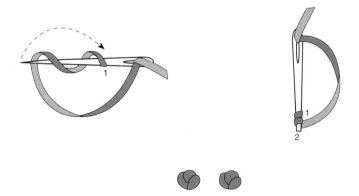

Bring needle up at 1 and wrap ribbon once or twice around shaft of needle. Swing point of needle clockwise and insert into fabric at 2, close to 1. Keep the working ribbon wrapped loosely around needle as you pull needle through to back of fabric. Release wrapping ribbon as knot is formed, and do not pull the knot too tightly. You can change the size of the French Knot by using different ribbon widths, wrapping the ribbon one or more times around needle, and/or varying your tension. For a larger knot, work a Colonial Knot (page 8).

Gathering Stitch

Thread needle with floss to match ribbon; knot end of floss. Work a series of small running stitches along one edge of ribbon. Pull thread to create desired density and knot thread to secure the gathering.

Lazy Daisy Stitches

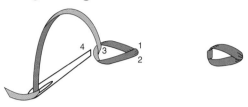

The basic Lazy Daisy Stitch is followed by two variations.

Lazy Daisy Stitch

Bring needle up at 1 and re-insert needle next to 1 (skipping a thread or two to avoid piercing the ribbon). Pull until the loop is desired length. Bring needle up at 3 with loop below point of needle. Pull ribbon through until desired shape is formed. Re-insert needle over the loop at 4 (close to 3) to anchor it.

Decorative Lazy Daisy Stitch

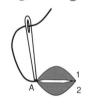

Make a Lazy Daisy Stitch (above), then use the same or contrasting color ribbon to work a Straight Stitch (page 12), coming up at A and down at B, inside the open area of the loop.

Modified Lazy Daisy Stitch

Using a wide ribbon, begin as for a Lazy Daisy Stitch (above), coming up at 1 and down at 2. Pull ribbon just enough to make a folded point. Use matching floss to tack point (A) in place and continue tacking to create desired shape. End off ribbon.

Loop Stitch

Bring needle up at 1, stitch down at 2, and pull ribbon part way through fabric. Insert a piece of drinking straw (or pencil, large tapestry needle, paper clip, etc.) through loop; pull ribbon snug to hold shape. Keep straw in place until the next loop is made in the same manner, then remove straw. If desired, these upright loops can be tacked in place.

Ribbon Stitches

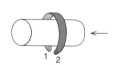

The basic Ribbon Stitch is followed by five variations.

Ribbon Stitch

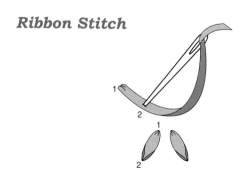

Bring needle up at 1 and flatten ribbon as it emerges through fabric. Extend ribbon just beyond length of stitch and insert needle through top of ribbon at 2. Pull ribbon gently through fabric as the sides of ribbon curl inward to form a point. Leave the curls showing by not pulling too tightly. Vary this stitch by using different ribbon widths and tension.

Modified Ribbon Stitch

This technique creates a Ribbon Stitch with a straight horizontal base. Bring ribbon out of fabric above intended bottom edge of stitch (1). Hold ribbon downward and use matching floss to tack each side to fabric (A and B). Bring ribbon upward and stitch down (2) to work remainder of the Ribbon Stitch in the usual manner; dotted line shows hidden beginning section of ribbon.

Padded Ribbon Stitch

Make a Colonial Knot (page 8), then make a Ribbon Stitch (page 10) centered over knot.

Twisted Ribbon Stitch

Begin at 1 as if to make a Ribbon Stitch (page 10), but give the ribbon a single twist before stitching down at 2 to create a point.

Side Ribbon Stitch

Begin at 1 as if to make a Ribbon Stitch (page 10), but insert needle close to one edge of ribbon at 2. Continue to pull gently until desired shape for tip is achieved.

Padded Side Ribbon Stitch

Make a French Knot (page 9), then make a Side Ribbon Stitch (above) centered over knot.

Spider Web

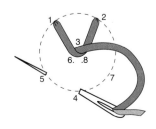

Begin by making an extended Fly Stitch (page 9) with a narrow ribbon or floss, extending the distance between 3 and 4. Add two extra legs (5-6 and 7-8) to create a base. End off ribbon. Bring a different ribbon up at center of web and begin weaving over and under the five legs in a circular manner until desired fullness is achieved. To end, insert needle beneath web and pull gently through fabric. Do not worry about twists—they add interest and dimension.

Stem Stitch

Bring needle up at 1. Use the thumb of your non-stitching hand to hold ribbon flat. Stitch down at 2 and up at 3, then pull the ribbon through. Continue in this manner, with ribbon held below stitching. Frequently, floss is used to work this stitch.

Straight Stitches

The basic Straight Stitch is followed by five variations.

Straight Stitch

Bring needle from back of fabric at beginning point of stitch at 1. Use non-stitching thumb and forefinger to keep ribbon from twisting as you stitch down at opposite end of stitch at 2. Pull gently from 1 to 2, keeping the stitch flat. This stitch can also be worked loosely, with some slack, if desired.

Padded Straight Stitch

Make a Straight Stitch (above), then work a longer Straight Stitch directly over the first one.

Modified Straight Stitch

This technique creates a Straight Stitch with straight ends. Bring ribbon out of fabric above intended bottom edge of stitch (1). Hold ribbon downward and use matching floss to tack each side to fabric (A and B). Bring ribbon upward and stitch down below intended top edge of stitch (2). Hold ribbon flat and use matching floss to tack each side down to fabric (C and D). Dotted lines show hidden beginning and ending sections of ribbon. Sometimes just the beginning of the Modified Straight Stitch is tacked down.

Modified Padded Straight Stitch

Make a basic Straight Stitch (above), then work a longer Modified Straight Stitch (above) directly over the first one. Dotted lines indicate the hidden first stitch and beginning of second stitch.

Twisted Straight Stitch

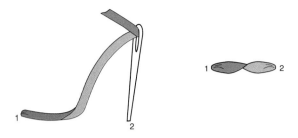

Bring needle up at 1, give ribbon a single twist, and stitch down at 2.

Padded Twisted Straight Stitch

Make two Colonial Knots (page 8), then make a Twisted Straight Stitch (above), bringing needle up through fabric at 1 and down at 2. Use matching floss to tack at center and as needed to retain shape. Dotted lines indicate hidden knots.

Tack Stitch

Tacking is a technique that invisibly anchors the ribbon in a desired position. Use one strand of floss to match the ribbon. Make one or more tiny straight stitches along edge of ribbon to create an indentation or retain a shape.

Weaving

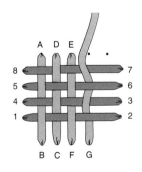

This technique can be used to fill any space. Follow numerical sequence to work horizontal Straight Stitches (page 12) for the foundation.
Bring a new ribbon up at A and weave over and under the previously worked stitches, making sure ribbon does not twist; stitch down at B. Weave additional rows in alternating patterns. Continue to fill space in this manner. The foundation can also be laid with diagonal stitches, weaving on the opposite diagonal.

Wrapped Bar

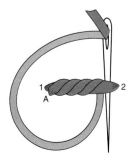

Make a Straight Stitch (page 12) of desired length (1-2). Then bring needle up at A, close to 1. Wrap the bar by slipping needle consecutively several times under the stitch; wrap to completely fill stitch. Stitch down into fabric to end.

Ribbon Color Conversion Key

Use this Color Conversion Key as a guide for choosing different brands of embroidery ribbon. We have included the following ribbon companies: Bucilla silk (76 colors), Offray Silk-Ease™ (56 colors), True Colors Silken™ (28 colors), Mokuba (Wright's) Heirloom Sylk™ (78 colors), and YLI silk (185 colors). These five companies have distinct color assortments that may not match each other, and the ribbon width selection also varies. The key below does not reflect the complete color range for each company; these are suggested substitutes for ribbons used in this book. Follow the stitching guides for the motifs as you refer to the color photos on pages 17-20 and the back cover; choose from the array of ribbons that is readily available to you.

	Bucilla	Mokuba	Offray	TC	YLI		Bucilla	Mokuba	Offray	TC	YLI
white	3	558	28	100	1	lt peach	516	74	215	50	166
ivory	501	470	810	101	156	med peach	516	74	215	51	87
lt pink	550	9	95	40	68	very lt orange	514	81	215	101	135
med pink	552	44	140	41	123	lt orange	514	102	215	50	39
dk pink	566	18	168	43	153	med orange	516	124	707	50	106
lt dusty pink	540	34	161	40	163	med dk orange	516	124	707	51	40
med dusty pink	553	35	168	41	158	dk orange	522	124	753	51	43
lt fuchsia	553	13	117	42	144	very lt yellow	655	470	617	101	13
med fuchsia	565	18	178	42	145	lt yellow	656	401	824	105	14
dk fuchsia	566	18	183	43	146	med yellow	666	424	645	106	15
lt rose	550	9	161	40	122	dk yellow	666	424	660	106	54
med rose	553	13	168	41	128	lt bright yellow	656	429	640	105	119
dk rose	553	39	169	42	129	med bright yellow	656	429	640	105	120
lt red	537	9	117	50	24	lt gold	655	470	617	101	12
med lt red	540	67	159	50	25	dk gold	666	445	745	106	52
med red	539	48	140	50	48	very lt yellow-green	509	367	513	1	154
med dk red	539	109	235	20	2	lt yellow-green	240	367	513	1	31
dk red	536	559	260	21	49	med lt yellow-green	545	356	581	*302	60
lt berry	537	71	117	50	7	med yellow-green	642	374	570	3	20
med lt berry	541	67	244	51	113	med dk yellow-green	643	366	570	4	72
med berry	553	29	775	43	114	dk yellow-green	617	379	571	6	21
med dk berry	562	112	235	20	92	lt olive green	509	374	567	3	170
dk berry	563	48	260	21	50	med olive green	240	364	570	5	56
very lt peach	531	23	203	50	5	dk olive green	20	366	571	4	171

For simplicity of description in our stitching guides, we have given generic names for the colors with the following abbreviations: lt (light), med (medium) and dk (dark). Refer to this key for the name of each color used for a motif, then look at the color range of your chosen brand and make adjustments as necessary. These color suggestions will produce a similar (but not identical) color scheme as the photographed samples. Occasionally, of necessity, numbers will be repeated; you can choose whether to use the same color or to substitute a different color value.

Color ranges vary greatly between companies, so you can really choose whatever colors you want based on what is readily available and your own personal preference.

	Bucilla	Mokuba	Offray	TC	YLI		Bucilla	Mokuba	Offray	TC	YLI
lt bright green	651	356	550	1	94	med orchid	568	143	430	93	23
med bright green	642	357	556	3	95	dk orchid	569	153	467	93	84
dk bright green	545	312	580	5	96	lt purple	24	162	430	92	101
lt green	615	317	530	*302	18	med purple	9	163	447	92	102
med green	638	340	584	5	19	dk purple	71	160	463	93	85
dk green	545	348	580	6	61	very dk purple	113	153	467	93	86
very lt gray-green	615	514	513	*304	155	violet	322	228	345	91	117
lt gray-green	615	317	513	*304	73	lt mauve	204	158	430	40	178
med lt gray-green	625	317	530	*302	74	dk mauve	568	178	467	41	177
med gray-green	617	360	564	*302	32	tan	655	37	810	101	35
dk gray-green	617	335	587	*302	33	lt brown	655	81	810	101	34
very lt turquoise	609	262	316	90	124	med brown	668	465	824	101	55
lt turquoise	607	287	316	*304	115	dk brown	668	468	846	94	36
med turquoise	607	317	327	*302	116	very dk brown	671	137	846	94	37
dk turquoise	608	317	327	*302	133	lt rust	503	37	824	94	161
lt aqua	609	312	314	90	132	med rust	668	468	824	94	172
dk aqua	608	336	323	*302	64	dk rust	668	137	846	94	79
lt blue	459	296	303	90	125	lt brick	531	37	824	94	6
med lt blue	600	204	303	90	44	med brick	524	468	824	94	112
med blue	322	352	332	80	126	dk brick	536	137	846	94	89
dk blue	585	228	345	80	82	taupe	501	137	824	94	65
lt bright blue	609	312	314	90	10	lt gray	3	535	28	100	58
dk bright blue	608	336	323	*302	11	med gray	668	600	435	94	30
lt orchid	204	141	434	92	22	black	002	600	30	120	4

*These colors are variegated ribbons; use the appropriate section of the ribbon.

Front Cover Stitching Key

The designs shown stitched on the front cover are listed below. The number on each project indicates the page number for that project's instructions. The project name is also listed for ease in location.

This assortment uses less than one-fifth of the designs in the book. All of the projects are shown stitched on the following four color pages and the back cover.

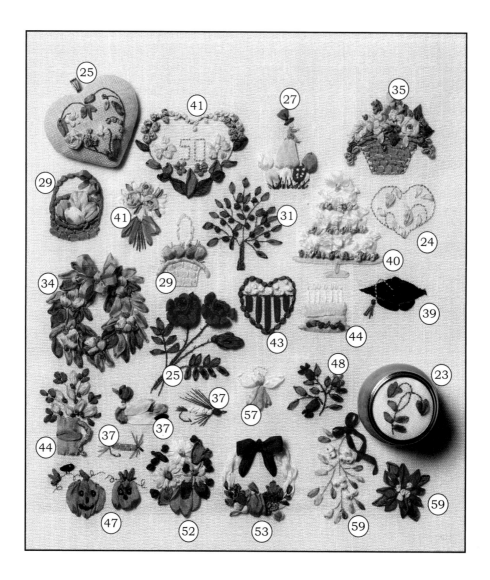

St. Valentine's Day

Hearts 'n Bows

Valentine

A

Chocolates

B

C

D

Double Heart Plant

Folk Heart A

Fleur Wreath

Heartstring

LOVE

Heart Posies

Bouquet of Roses

Folk
Heart B

Hearts 'n Hearts

Folk Heart C

St. Patrick's Day

Shamrock A

Shamrock Plant

Leprechaun Hat

Shamrock B

Rainbow

Leprechaun & Toadstools

IRISH

IRISH

Easter

Cross

Calla Lily

Easter Basket
with Bow

Chick

Easter Basket

Rabbit Face

Decorated Easter Eggs

Spring
Blossom

A

B

Bunny

Carrot Bunch

Arbor Day

Topiary Trees

Pine Tree

Fruit Tree

Spruce Tree

Deciduous Tree

Potted Topiary

Mother's Day

Sewing Basket

Wreath

Tulip Bouquet

Roses for Mother

Elegant Bouquet

MOM

Country Bouquet

Yellow Tulips

Orange Topiary

Father's Day

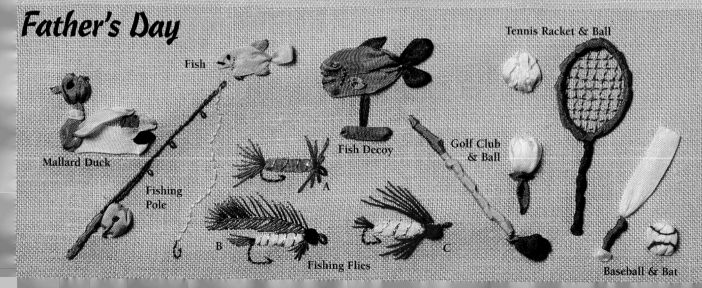

Tennis Racket & Ball

Fish

Mallard Duck

Fishing Pole

Fishing Flies

Fish Decoy

Golf Club & Ball

Baseball & Bat

Graduation

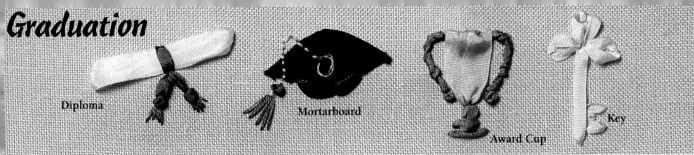

Diploma

Mortarboard

Award Cup

Key

Wedding & Anniversary

Intertwined Rings

Anniversary

Wedding Bells

Wedding Cake

Bridal Bouquet

Anniversary Bouquet

Fourth of July

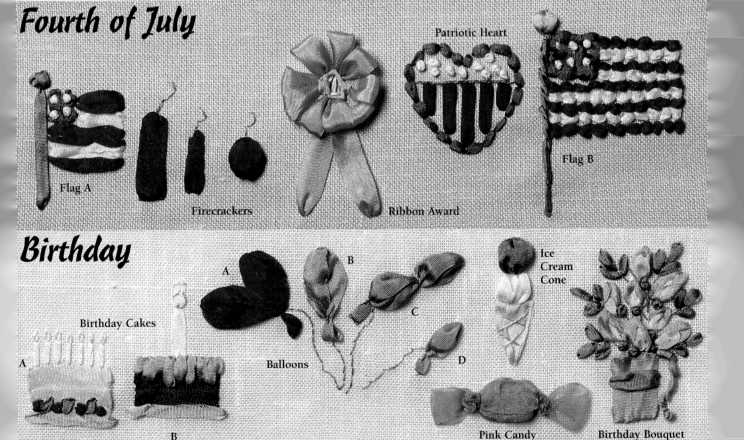

Flag A

Firecrackers

Ribbon Award

Patriotic Heart

Flag B

Birthday

Birthday Cakes

A

B

A

B

C

D

Balloons

Ice Cream Cone

Pink Candy

Birthday Bouquet

Halloween

Bat A

Jack-O'-Lantern A

Jack-O'-Lantern B

Bat B

Guess Who!

BOO!

Black Cat

Spider

Judaic

Wheat

7 Species with Hai

Pomegranate

Star of David

Menorah

Dreidl

Small Star of David

Sukkah

Hallah

Holiday Designs

The holiday designs are sorted by category on pages 22-60. The table of contents on page three of this book lists the categories and page numbers. The back cover and the color plates on pages 17-20 show a sample of each design in the book, grouped by category, and have the name of each project for your convenience. The drawings for each project shows the ribbon size and color and the stitches used for the photographed samples. Refer to the key on pages 14 and 15 for color suggestions using different manufacturers' brands.

Six-strand cotton embroidery floss is sometimes used for stems, knots, or small design details. Unless otherwise directed, use two strands of floss. For stems, leaves, and tendrils, choose a color value that complements the greenery. For other design details, refer to the generic color name listed on the drawing and select a color value of your favorite brand of floss.

St. Valentine's Day

Hearts 'n Bows

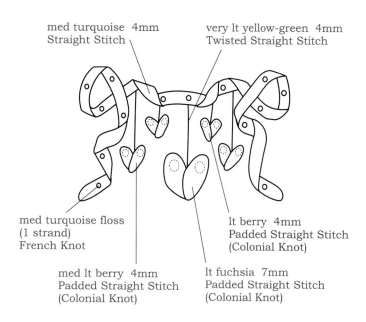

med turquoise 4mm
Straight Stitch

very lt yellow-green 4mm
Twisted Straight Stitch

med turquoise floss
(1 strand)
French Knot

lt berry 4mm
Padded Straight Stitch
(Colonial Knot)

med lt berry 4mm
Padded Straight Stitch
(Colonial Knot)

lt fuchsia 7mm
Padded Straight Stitch
(Colonial Knot)

Stitching order:
For the bow, work one long Straight Stitch in a curved and looped design; use floss to work French Knots to attach ribbon and hold desired shape. For heart hangers, work five Twisted Straight Stitches in various lengths. At each end, work a heart with two Padded Straight Stitches (Straight Stitch over Colonial Knot).

Chocolates

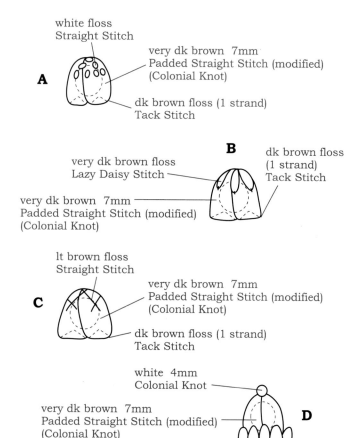

white floss
Straight Stitch

very dk brown 7mm
Padded Straight Stitch (modified)
(Colonial Knot)

A

dk brown floss (1 strand)
Tack Stitch

very dk brown floss
Lazy Daisy Stitch

B

dk brown floss
(1 strand)
Tack Stitch

very dk brown 7mm
Padded Straight Stitch (modified)
(Colonial Knot)

lt brown floss
Straight Stitch

C

very dk brown 7mm
Padded Straight Stitch (modified)
(Colonial Knot)

dk brown floss (1 strand)
Tack Stitch

white 4mm
Colonial Knot

very dk brown 7mm
Padded Straight Stitch (modified)
(Colonial Knot)

D

lt brown 4mm
Straight Stitch

Stitching order:
Basic Candy
For basic candy, work two modified Padded Straight Stitches (Straight Stitch over loose Colonial Knot).

Version A
Work basic candy. Use floss to work tiny Straight Stitches on top.

Version B
Work basic candy. Use floss to work three Lazy Daisies on top.

Version C
Work basic candy. Use floss to Straight Stitch crosshatch design on top.

Version D
Work basic candy. Work five Straight Stitches at bottom of candy for wrapper and top with a Colonial Knot.

Valentine

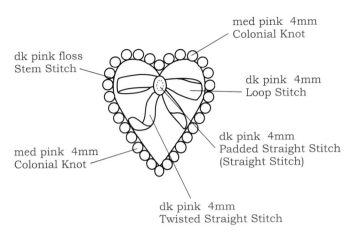

med pink 4mm
Colonial Knot

dk pink floss
Stem Stitch

dk pink 4mm
Loop Stitch

dk pink 4mm
Padded Straight Stitch
(Straight Stitch)

med pink 4mm
Colonial Knot

dk pink 4mm
Twisted Straight Stitch

Stitching order:
Use floss to work Stem Stitch in shape of a heart. Add Colonial Knots around outside of shape. At top center, work bow with two Loop Stitches, a Padded Straight Stitch (Straight Stitch over Straight Stitch) for knot, and two Twisted Straight Stitches for streamers.

Folk Hearts

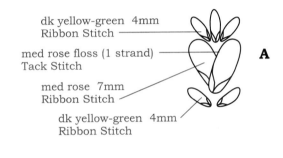

dk yellow-green 4mm
Ribbon Stitch

med rose floss (1 strand)
Tack Stitch

med rose 7mm
Ribbon Stitch

dk yellow-green 4mm
Ribbon Stitch

A

Stitching order:
Version A
Work two overlapping Ribbon Stitches; tack with floss to form heart shape. Work three Ribbon Stitch leaves at top and two Ribbon Stitch leaves at base.

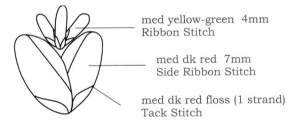

med yellow-green 4mm
Ribbon Stitch

med dk red 7mm
Side Ribbon Stitch

med dk red floss (1 strand)
Tack Stitch

B

Version B
Work two pairs of overlapping Side Ribbon Stitches. Work three Ribbon Stitch leaves at top.

lt pink 4mm
Ribbon Stitch

lt bright green 4mm
Ribbon Stitch

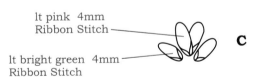

C

Version C
Work two overlapping Ribbon Stitches. Work two Ribbon Stitch leaves at base.

Double Heart Plant

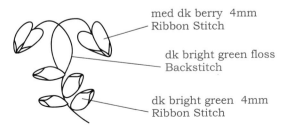

med dk berry 4mm
Ribbon Stitch

dk bright green floss
Backstitch

dk bright green 4mm
Ribbon Stitch

Stitching order:
Use floss to Backstitch curved stems. Work four Ribbon Stitch leaves on lower part of stem. For each flower, work two overlapping Ribbon Stitches.

Heartstring

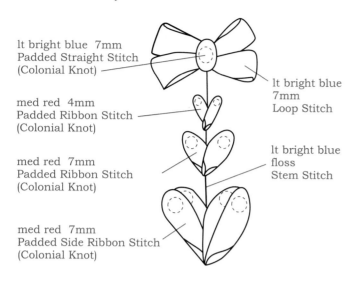

lt bright blue 7mm
Padded Straight Stitch
(Colonial Knot)

med red 4mm
Padded Ribbon Stitch
(Colonial Knot)

med red 7mm
Padded Ribbon Stitch
(Colonial Knot)

med red 7mm
Padded Side Ribbon Stitch
(Colonial Knot)

lt bright blue
7mm
Loop Stitch

lt bright blue
floss
Stem Stitch

Stitching order:

Use floss to Stem Stitch a vertical line. At top, work four Loop Stitches, with a Padded Straight Stitch (Straight Stitch over Colonial Knot) at center. For each of the top two hearts, work two overlapping Padded Ribbon Stitches (Ribbon Stitch over Colonial Knot). For the lower heart, work two pairs of overlapping Padded Side Ribbon Stitches (Side Ribbon Stitch over Colonial Knot).

Love

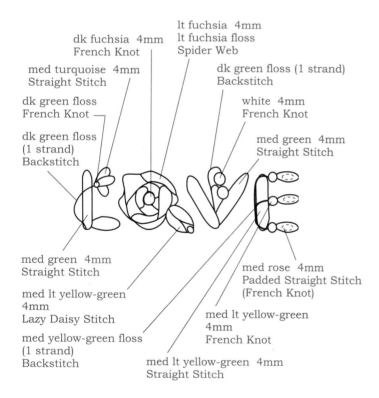

dk fuchsia 4mm
French Knot

med turquoise 4mm
Straight Stitch

dk green floss
French Knot

dk green floss
(1 strand)
Backstitch

lt fuchsia 4mm
lt fuchsia floss
Spider Web

dk green floss (1 strand)
Backstitch

white 4mm
French Knot

med green 4mm
Straight Stitch

med green 4mm
Straight Stitch

med lt yellow-green
4mm
Lazy Daisy Stitch

med yellow-green floss
(1 strand)
Backstitch

med rose 4mm
Padded Straight Stitch
(French Knot)

med lt yellow-green
4mm
French Knot

med lt yellow-green 4mm
Straight Stitch

Stitching order:

For the "L," work two Straight Stitches. Use floss to Backstitch stem. Work three Straight Stitches for flower, using floss for French Knot center.

For the "O," work a Spider Web with a French Knot at center. Work a Lazy Daisy leaf at lower right.

For the "V," work two Straight Stitches. Use floss to Backstitch stems. Work two French Knots for flowers.

For the "E," work a Straight Stitch. Use floss to Backstitch stems. At end of each stem, work a French Knot then a Padded Srraight Stitch (Straight Stitch over French Knot).

Hearts 'n Hearts

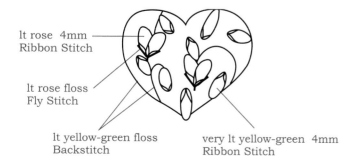

lt rose 4mm
Ribbon Stitch

lt rose floss
Fly Stitch

lt yellow-green floss
Backstitch

very lt yellow-green 4mm
Ribbon Stitch

Stitching order:

Use floss to work Backstitch in shape of a heart; add stems as shown. Work Ribbon Stitch leaves and two pairs of overlapping Ribbon Stitches for flowers. At bottom tip of each flower, use floss to add a Fly Stitch.

Fleur Wreath

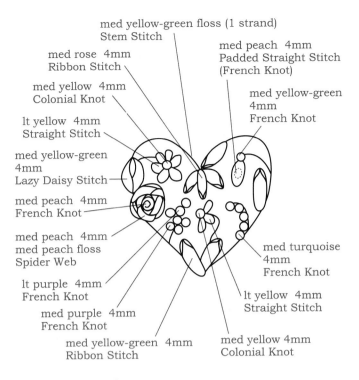

med yellow-green floss (1 strand)
Stem Stitch

med rose 4mm
Ribbon Stitch

med yellow 4mm
Colonial Knot

lt yellow 4mm
Straight Stitch

med yellow-green
4mm
Lazy Daisy Stitch

med peach 4mm
French Knot

med peach 4mm
med peach floss
Spider Web

lt purple 4mm
French Knot

med purple 4mm
French Knot

med yellow-green 4mm
Ribbon Stitch

med peach 4mm
Padded Straight Stitch
(French Knot)

med yellow-green
4mm
French Knot

med turquoise
4mm
French Knot

lt yellow 4mm
Straight Stitch

med yellow 4mm
Colonial Knot

Stitching order:
Use floss to Stem Stitch a heart shape, adding flower stems as shown. Work Lazy Daisy and Ribbon Stitch leaves. At top center, work a flower with three Ribbon Stitch petals, working the center one on top. At upper right, work a Padded Straight Stitch (Straight Stitch over French Knot) topped with a French Knot. At lower right, work French Knots along stem. At center, work a flower with three Straight Stitch petals topped with a Colonial Knot. At lower left, work French Knots in two colors on each side of stem. Below Lazy Daisy leaf, work a Spider Web Rose with a French Knot at center. Above this flower, work six Straight Stitches with a Colonial Knot at center.

Bouquet of Roses

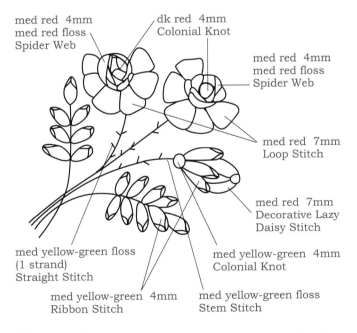

med red 4mm
med red floss
Spider Web

dk red 4mm
Colonial Knot

med red 4mm
med red floss
Spider Web

med red 7mm
Loop Stitch

med red 7mm
Decorative Lazy
Daisy Stitch

med yellow-green floss
(1 strand)
Straight Stitch

med yellow-green 4mm
Ribbon Stitch

med yellow-green 4mm
Colonial Knot

med yellow-green floss
Stem Stitch

Stitching order:
Use floss to work Stem Stitch stems; add Straight Stitch thorns along the three center stems. For each full bloom, work a Spider Web (with center of spokes toward top of blossom) with a Colonial Knot at center; for petals, work five or six Loop Stitches, overlapping top of stem. For the bud, work a Decorative Lazy Daisy; add three Ribbon Stitches and a Colonial Knot. Work Ribbon Stitch leaves on remaining stems.

Heart Posies

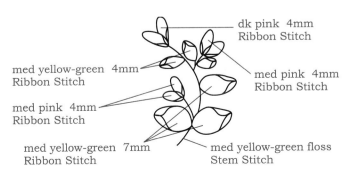

med yellow-green 4mm
Ribbon Stitch

med pink 4mm
Ribbon Stitch

med yellow-green 7mm
Ribbon Stitch

dk pink 4mm
Ribbon Stitch

med pink 4mm
Ribbon Stitch

med yellow-green floss
Stem Stitch

Stitching order:
Use floss to Stem Stitch curved stems. Work Ribbon Stitch leaves along each stem. For each flower, work two overlapping Ribbon Stitches.

St. Patrick's Day

Shamrock Plant

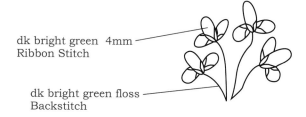

dk bright green 4mm
Ribbon Stitch

dk bright green floss
Backstitch

Stitching order:
Use floss to Backstitch stems; work three Ribbon Stitches for each group of petals.

Shamrocks

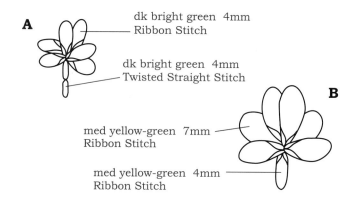

A

dk bright green 4mm
Ribbon Stitch

dk bright green 4mm
Twisted Straight Stitch

B

med yellow-green 7mm
Ribbon Stitch

med yellow-green 4mm
Ribbon Stitch

Stitching order:
Version A
Work stem with a Twisted Straight Stitch. Work three pairs of Ribbon Stitches for petals.

Version B
Work stem with a Ribbon Stitch. Work three pairs of Ribbon Stitches for petals.

Leprechaun Hat

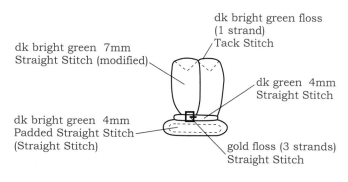

dk bright green floss
(1 strand)
Tack Stitch

dk bright green 7mm
Straight Stitch (modified)

dk green 4mm
Straight Stitch

dk bright green 4mm
Padded Straight Stitch
(Straight Stitch)

gold floss (3 strands)
Straight Stitch

Stitching order:
Work two modified Straight Stitches for the hat top. Across bottom work a Straight Stitch for hatband then a Padded Straight Stitch (Straight Stitch over Straight Stitch) for the brim. Use floss to Straight Stitch buckle on hatband.

Rainbow

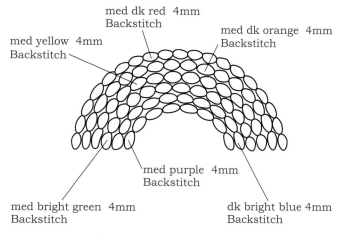

med dk red 4mm
Backstitch

med dk orange 4mm
Backstitch

med yellow 4mm
Backstitch

med purple 4mm
Backstitch

med bright green 4mm
Backstitch

dk bright blue 4mm
Backstitch

Stitching order:
Beginning with top edge of rainbow, work rows of Backstitch in an arc.

26

Irish

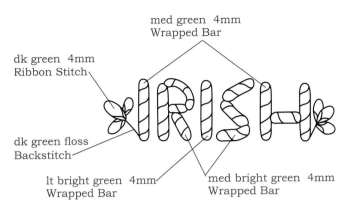

med green 4mm
Wrapped Bar

dk green 4mm
Ribbon Stitch

dk green floss
Backstitch

lt bright green 4mm
Wrapped Bar

med bright green 4mm
Wrapped Bar

Stitching order:
Work each letter with Wrapped Bars. Work each shamrock with three Ribbon Stitches and use floss to Backstitch stems.

Leprechaun & Toadstools

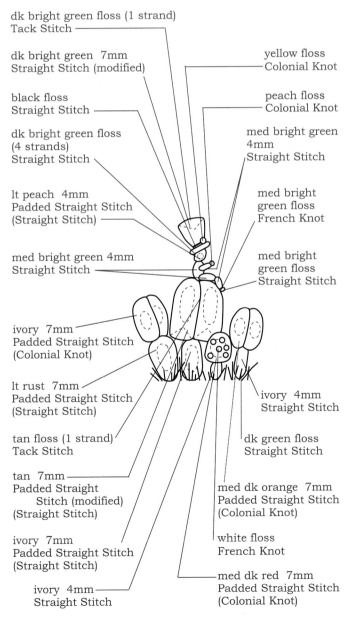

dk bright green floss (1 strand)
Tack Stitch

dk bright green 7mm
Straight Stitch (modified)

black floss
Straight Stitch

dk bright green floss
(4 strands)
Straight Stitch

lt peach 4mm
Padded Straight Stitch
(Straight Stitch)

med bright green 4mm
Straight Stitch

ivory 7mm
Padded Straight Stitch
(Colonial Knot)

lt rust 7mm
Padded Straight Stitch
(Straight Stitch)

tan floss (1 strand)
Tack Stitch

tan 7mm
Padded Straight
Stitch (modified)
(Straight Stitch)

ivory 7mm
Padded Straight Stitch
(Straight Stitch)

ivory 4mm
Straight Stitch

yellow floss
Colonial Knot

peach floss
Colonial Knot

med bright green
4mm
Straight Stitch

med bright
green floss
French Knot

med bright
green floss
Straight Stitch

ivory 4mm
Straight Stitch

dk green floss
Straight Stitch

med dk orange 7mm
Padded Straight Stitch
(Colonial Knot)

white floss
French Knot

med dk red 7mm
Padded Straight Stitch
(Colonial Knot)

Stitching order:
For large toadstool, work a Padded Straight Stitch (Straight Stitch over Straight Stitch) for the stem; work two modified Padded Straight Stitches (Straight Stitch over Straight Stitch) for the top. For left toadstool, work the stem in the same manner as large toadstool; work two Padded Straight Stitches (Straight Stitch over Colonial Knot) for the top. For two remaining toadstools, work a Straight Stitch for each stem and one or two Padded Straight Stitches (Straight Stitch over Colonial Knot) for top. On the shortest toadstool, work six French Knots on the top. Use floss to Straight Stitch grass over stems.

For leprechaun, work back, upper leg, lower leg, and arm with Straight Stitches. Use floss to work a French Knot and Straight Stitch for foot. Work a Padded Straight Stitch (Straight Stitch over Straight Stitch) for head, and use floss to work a Colonial Knot for hand. Work a modified Straight Stitch topped with floss Straight Stitches and a Colonial Knot for hat; use floss to work Straight Stitches for brim.

Easter

Cross

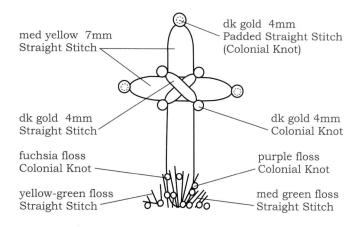

med yellow 7mm
Straight Stitch

dk gold 4mm
Padded Straight Stitch
(Colonial Knot)

dk gold 4mm
Straight Stitch

dk gold 4mm
Colonial Knot

fuchsia floss
Colonial Knot

purple floss
Colonial Knot

yellow-green floss
Straight Stitch

med green floss
Straight Stitch

Stitching order:
Work a long vertical Straight Stitch; a little above the middle work a horizontal Straight Stitch. For the three end knobs, work Padded Straight Stitches (Straight Stitch over Colonial Knot). Over center of cross work two Straight Stitches forming an "x"; work four Colonial Knots at corners of "x." At bottom of cross, use different colors of floss to work randomly placed Straight Stitches for grass and Colonial Knots for flowers.

Calla Lily

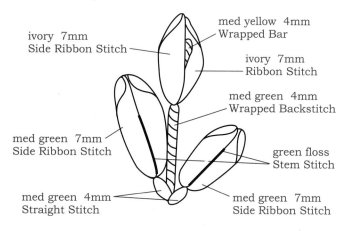

ivory 7mm
Side Ribbon Stitch

med yellow 4mm
Wrapped Bar

ivory 7mm
Ribbon Stitch

med green 4mm
Wrapped Backstitch

med green 7mm
Side Ribbon Stitch

green floss
Stem Stitch

med green 4mm
Straight Stitch

med green 7mm
Side Ribbon Stitch

Stitching order:
For main stem, work Wrapped Backstitch. For each leaf, work a short Straight Stitch for lower segment and two Side Ribbon Stitches for upper segment. Use floss to Stem Stitch veins. For flower, work a Ribbon Stitch with a Wrapped Bar for stamen; add a Side Ribbon Stitch over left edge of flower and tack if needed to retain shape.

Rabbit Face

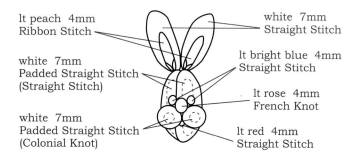

lt peach 4mm
Ribbon Stitch

white 7mm
Straight Stitch

white 7mm
Padded Straight Stitch
(Straight Stitch)

lt bright blue 4mm
Straight Stitch

lt rose 4mm
French Knot

white 7mm
Padded Straight Stitch
(Colonial Knot)

lt red 4mm
Straight Stitch

Stitching order:
For head, work two, three, or four Padded Straight Stitches (Straight Stitch over Straight Stitch) to fill space. Top with two Straight Stitches for eyes, a French Knot for the nose, a Straight Stitch for the mouth, and two Padded Straight Stitches (Straight Stitch over Colonial Knot) for cheeks. Work two Straight Stitches, each topped with a Ribbon Stitch for ears.

Chick

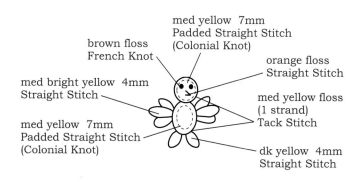

med yellow 7mm
Padded Straight Stitch
(Colonial Knot)

brown floss
French Knot

orange floss
Straight Stitch

med bright yellow 4mm
Straight Stitch

med yellow floss
(1 strand)
Tack Stitch

med yellow 7mm
Padded Straight Stitch
(Colonial Knot)

dk yellow 4mm
Straight Stitch

Stitching order:
For body, work a Padded Straight Stitch (Straight Stitch over loose Colonial Knot). For head, work a Padded Straight Stitch (Straight Stitch over Colonial Knot). Use floss to work two French Knots for eyes and Straight Stitches for beak. Tack sides of head and body to retain shape. For each wing, work three Straight Stitches (sides first, then middle one on top). For feet, work two Straight Stitches.

Easter Basket With Bow

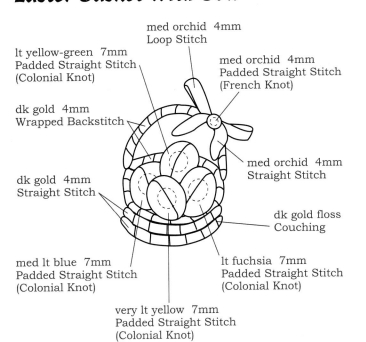

med orchid 4mm
Loop Stitch

lt yellow-green 7mm
Padded Straight Stitch
(Colonial Knot)

med orchid 4mm
Padded Straight Stitch
(French Knot)

dk gold 4mm
Wrapped Backstitch

med orchid 4mm
Straight Stitch

dk gold 4mm
Straight Stitch

dk gold floss
Couching

med lt blue 7mm
Padded Straight Stitch
(Colonial Knot)

lt fuchsia 7mm
Padded Straight Stitch
(Colonial Knot)

very lt yellow 7mm
Padded Straight Stitch
(Colonial Knot)

Stitching order:
Work closely spaced loose horizontal Straight Stitches for front of basket. Couch these stitches along curve with floss, working vertical stitches in an alternating pattern to simulate a woven design. Work Wrapped Backstitch for handle and rim of basket. For eggs, work four Padded Straight Stitches (two Straight Stitches over a Colonial Knot), overlapping basket edges. For bow, work two Loop Stitches on handle with a Padded Straight Stitch (Straight Stitch over French Knot) at center. Add two Straight Stitches for streamers.

Easter Basket

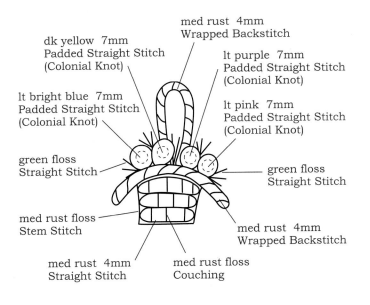

dk yellow 7mm
Padded Straight Stitch
(Colonial Knot)

med rust 4mm
Wrapped Backstitch

lt purple 7mm
Padded Straight Stitch
(Colonial Knot)

lt bright blue 7mm
Padded Straight Stitch
(Colonial Knot)

lt pink 7mm
Padded Straight Stitch
(Colonial Knot)

green floss
Straight Stitch

green floss
Straight Stitch

med rust floss
Stem Stitch

med rust 4mm
Wrapped Backstitch

med rust 4mm
Straight Stitch

med rust floss
Couching

Stitching order:
Work closely spaced horizontal Straight Stitches for basket. Couch these stitches with floss, working vertical stitches in an alternating pattern to simulate a woven design. Work Stem Stitch with floss on both sides and bottom. Work Wrapped Backstitch for rim, extending edges, and also for handle. For eggs, work four Padded Straight Stitches (Straight Stitch over Colonial Knot) in desired color arrangement. Use floss to Straight Stitch the grass.

Spring Blossom

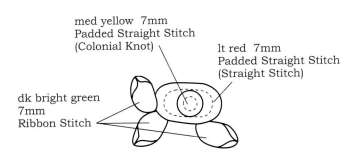

med yellow 7mm
Padded Straight Stitch
(Colonial Knot)

lt red 7mm
Padded Straight Stitch
(Straight Stitch)

dk bright green
7mm
Ribbon Stitch

Stitching order:
For flower, work a Padded Straight Stitch (Straight Stitch over Straight Stitch), topped with a Padded Straight Stitch (Straight Stitch over Colonial Knot). For leaves, work Ribbon Stitches, beginning under edges of flower.

Decorated Easter Eggs

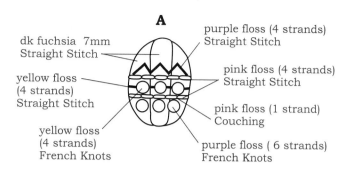

A

dk fuchsia 7mm
Straight Stitch

purple floss (4 strands)
Straight Stitch

yellow floss
(4 strands)
Straight Stitch

pink floss (4 strands)
Straight Stitch

yellow floss
(4 strands)
French Knots

pink floss (1 strand)
Couching

purple floss (6 strands)
French Knots

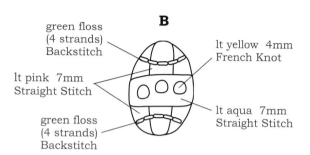

B

green floss
(4 strands)
Backstitch

lt yellow 4mm
French Knot

lt pink 7mm
Straight Stitch

green floss
(4 strands)
Backstitch

lt aqua 7mm
Straight Stitch

Stitching order:

Version A

For basic egg, work three vertical Straight Stitches, one on each side and the third (longer) one on top, keeping bottom edge flatter than top. For center trim, use floss to work Straight Stitches connected with French Knots. Above and below this line, use floss to Couch the Straight Stitches. Above band, work floss Straight Stitches in a zigzag design, and below band work three French Knots with floss.

Version B

For basic egg, work as for Version A. For trim, work a horizontal Straight Stitch, beginning beneath side of egg and ending under opposite side of egg; top with three French Knots. Use floss to Backstitch above and below center band.

Bunny

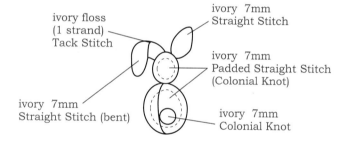

ivory floss
(1 strand)
Tack Stitch

ivory 7mm
Straight Stitch

ivory 7mm
Padded Straight Stitch
(Colonial Knot)

ivory 7mm
Straight Stitch (bent)

ivory 7mm
Colonial Knot

Stitching order:

For body, work two Padded Straight Stitches (Straight Stitch over Colonial Knot) topped with a Colonial Knot near bottom for tail. For head, work Padded Straight Stitch (Straight Stitch over Colonial Knot). Work a Straight Stitch for right ear. Work a Straight Stitch for bent ear in the following manner. Bring ribbon up at base of head and place flat as if to work a Straight Stitch; use matching floss to tack ear to fabric the desired distance from head, fold ribbon forward (hiding the tacking stitch), and enter fabric at desired location.

Carrot Bunch

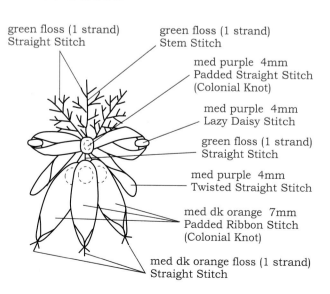

green floss (1 strand)
Straight Stitch

green floss (1 strand)
Stem Stitch

med purple 4mm
Padded Straight Stitch
(Colonial Knot)

med purple 4mm
Lazy Daisy Stitch

green floss (1 strand)
Straight Stitch

med purple 4mm
Twisted Straight Stitch

med dk orange 7mm
Padded Ribbon Stitch
(Colonial Knot)

med dk orange floss (1 strand)
Straight Stitch

Stitching order:

For carrots, work three Padded Ribbon Stitches (Ribbon Stitch over Colonial Knot) with the center one on top; work Straight Stitches with floss for rootlets. Use floss to Stem Stitch stems, filling in with Straight Stitches. For bow, work two Lazy Daisies with a Padded Straight Stitch (Straight Stitch over Colonial Knot) at center and two Twisted Straight Stitches for streamers.

Arbor Day

Topiary Tree

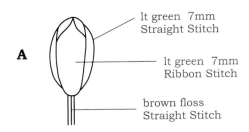

lt green 7mm
Straight Stitch

lt green 7mm
Ribbon Stitch

brown floss
Straight Stitch

Stitching order:

Version A
Work two Straight Stitches next to each other, then work a Ribbon Stitch on top. Use floss to work Straight Stitch stem.

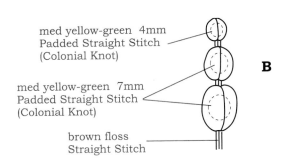

med yellow-green 4mm
Padded Straight Stitch
(Colonial Knot)

med yellow-green 7mm
Padded Straight Stitch
(Colonial Knot)

brown floss
Straight Stitch

Version B
Work three Padded Straight Stitches (two Straight Stitches over a Colonial Knot). Use floss to work Straight Stitch stem between padded stitches.

Pine Tree

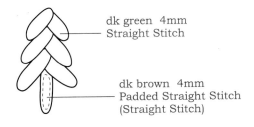

dk green 4mm
Straight Stitch

dk brown 4mm
Padded Straight Stitch
(Straight Stitch)

Stitching order:
Work Padded Straight Stitch (Straight Stitch over Straight Stitch) for trunk. Beginning at the bottom work overlapping Straight Stitches for branches.

Fruit Tree

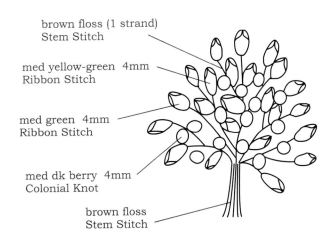

brown floss (1 strand)
Stem Stitch

med yellow-green 4mm
Ribbon Stitch

med green 4mm
Ribbon Stitch

med dk berry 4mm
Colonial Knot

brown floss
Stem Stitch

Stitching order:
Use floss to work trunk in Stem Stitch, working outward toward bottom. Work Stem Stitch branches, Ribbon Stitch leaves in alternating colors, and Colonial Knots for fruit.

Spruce Tree

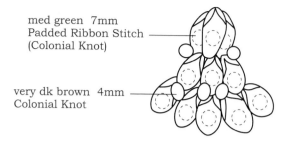

med green 7mm
Padded Ribbon Stitch
(Colonial Knot)

very dk brown 4mm
Colonial Knot

Stitching order:
Work Padded Ribbon Stitches (Ribbon Stitch over Colonial Knot) in the shape of a triangle from bottom up, finishing with the last stitch centered at top. Add Colonial Knots for pinecones.

Deciduous Tree

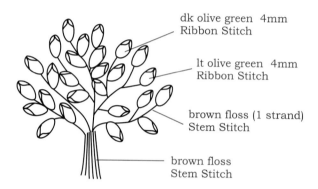

dk olive green 4mm
Ribbon Stitch

lt olive green 4mm
Ribbon Stitch

brown floss (1 strand)
Stem Stitch

brown floss
Stem Stitch

Stitching order:
Use floss to work trunk in Stem Stitches, working outward toward bottom. Work Stem Stitch branches, and fill in with Ribbon Stitch leaves in alternating colors.

Potted Topiary

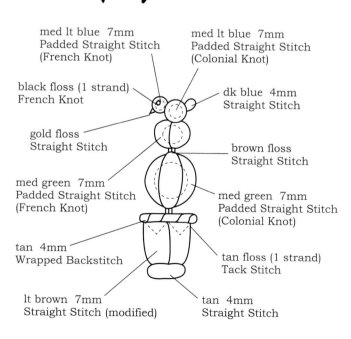

med lt blue 7mm
Padded Straight Stitch
(French Knot)

med lt blue 7mm
Padded Straight Stitch
(Colonial Knot)

black floss (1 strand)
French Knot

dk blue 4mm
Straight Stitch

gold floss
Straight Stitch

brown floss
Straight Stitch

med green 7mm
Padded Straight Stitch
(French Knot)

med green 7mm
Padded Straight Stitch
(Colonial Knot)

tan 4mm
Wrapped Backstitch

tan floss (1 strand)
Tack Stitch

lt brown 7mm
Straight Stitch (modified)

tan 4mm
Straight Stitch

Stitching order:
Work two modified Straight Stitches for vase; work a horizontal Straight Stitch for base, and a Wrapped Backstitch for rim. Slightly above vase, work Padded Straight Stitch (three Straight Stitches over a Colonial Knot) for lower globe. Slightly above that, work Padded Straight Stitch (two Straight Stitches over a French Knot) for upper globe. For bird, work a Padded Straight Stitch (Straight Stitch over Colonial Knot), a Straight Stitch, and a Padded Straight Stitch (Straight Stitch over French Knot). Use floss to work a French Knot for eye and Straight Stitch the beak and stems.

Mother's Day

Sewing Basket

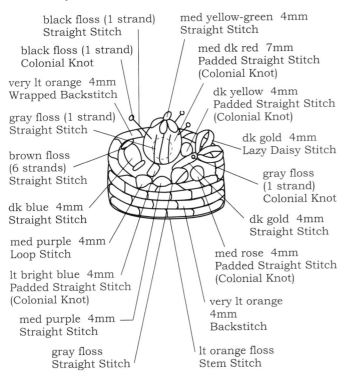

black floss (1 strand)
Straight Stitch

black floss (1 strand)
Colonial Knot

very lt orange 4mm
Wrapped Backstitch

gray floss (1 strand)
Straight Stitch

brown floss
(6 strands)
Straight Stitch

dk blue 4mm
Straight Stitch

med purple 4mm
Loop Stitch

lt bright blue 4mm
Padded Straight Stitch
(Colonial Knot)

med purple 4mm
Straight Stitch

gray floss
Straight Stitch

med yellow-green 4mm
Straight Stitch

med dk red 7mm
Padded Straight Stitch
(Colonial Knot)

dk yellow 4mm
Padded Straight Stitch
(Colonial Knot)

dk gold 4mm
Lazy Daisy Stitch

gray floss
(1 strand)
Colonial Knot

dk gold 4mm
Straight Stitch

med rose 4mm
Padded Straight Stitch
(Colonial Knot)

very lt orange
4mm
Backstitch

lt orange floss
Stem Stitch

Stitching order:

For basket, work three rows of Backstitches, curving slightly; for rim, work Wrapped Backstitch. Use floss to Stem Stitch basket outline. For the pincushion, work two Padded Straight Stitches (Straight Stitch over Colonial Knot) covered with two floss Straight Stitches. At top of pincushion, work three Straight Stitches topped with another Straight Stitch. For pins, work three Straight Stitches, each topped with a Colonial Knot.

For scissors, work one Straight Stitch for blades and (with ribbon tightly twisted) two Lazy Daisies for handles; use floss to work a Colonial Knot for hinge. For the floss skein, work a Loop Stitch, a Straight Stitch, and another Loop Stitch; use floss to work short Straight Stitches over joints. For spool, work a Straight Stitch and use floss to work Straight Stitches at each end. Fill in with Padded Straight Stitches (Straight Stitch over Colonial Knot) in desired colors.

Yellow Tulips

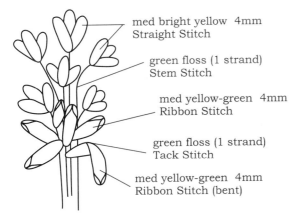

med bright yellow 4mm
Straight Stitch

green floss (1 strand)
Stem Stitch

med yellow-green 4mm
Ribbon Stitch

green floss (1 strand)
Tack Stitch

med yellow-green 4mm
Ribbon Stitch (bent)

Stitching order:

Use floss to Stem Stitch stems. For flowers, work Straight Stitches in groups of three. For leaves, work Ribbon Stitches, with a bent one near bottom. To make a bent leaf, refer to "Bunny" on page 30.

Roses For Mother

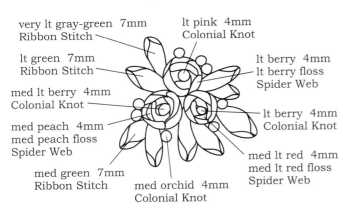

very lt gray-green 7mm
Ribbon Stitch

lt green 7mm
Ribbon Stitch

med lt berry 4mm
Colonial Knot

med peach 4mm
med peach floss
Spider Web

med green 7mm
Ribbon Stitch

med orchid 4mm
Colonial Knot

lt pink 4mm
Colonial Knot

lt berry 4mm
lt berry floss
Spider Web

lt berry 4mm
Colonial Knot

med lt red 4mm
med lt red floss
Spider Web

Stitching order:

Work three Spider Web Roses in different colors; work a Colonial Knot at each center. Work Ribbon Stitch leaves in different colors. Work Colonial Knots randomly placed between leaves and around roses.

Elegant Bouquet

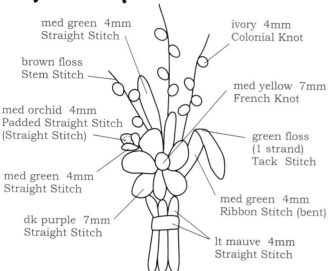

med green 4mm
Straight Stitch

brown floss
Stem Stitch

med orchid 4mm
Padded Straight Stitch
(Straight Stitch)

med green 4mm
Straight Stitch

dk purple 7mm
Straight Stitch

ivory 4mm
Colonial Knot

med yellow 7mm
French Knot

green floss
(1 strand)
Tack Stitch

med green 4mm
Ribbon Stitch (bent)

lt mauve 4mm
Straight Stitch

Stitching order:
For vase, work three vertical Straight Stitches, fanning out slightly at top; work a horizontal Straight Stitch above middle. Above vase, work two Straight Stitch leaves at center and a bent leaf on the right side; to make a bent stitch refer to "Bunny" on page 30. For flower, work six loose Straight Stitches overlapping the leaves; at center, work a French Knot. For bud, work a Padded Straight Stitch (Straight Stitch over Straight Stitch) overlapped with two Straight Stitch leaves. To make pussywillows, use floss to Stem Stitch stems, then work Colonial Knots alternately along both sides.

Orange Topiary

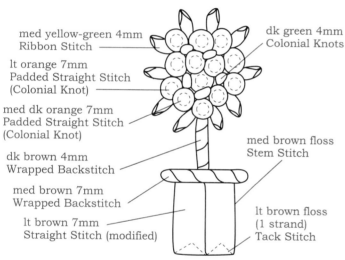

med yellow-green 4mm
Ribbon Stitch

lt orange 7mm
Padded Straight Stitch
(Colonial Knot)

med dk orange 7mm
Padded Straight Stitch
(Colonial Knot)

dk brown 4mm
Wrapped Backstitch

med brown 7mm
Wrapped Backstitch

lt brown 7mm
Straight Stitch (modified)

dk green 4mm
Colonial Knots

med brown floss
Stem Stitch

lt brown floss
(1 strand)
Tack Stitch

Stitching order:
To make container, work two modified Straight Stitches, using floss to tack down edges and Stem Stitch outline. Work rim and trunk in Wrapped Backstitch. Work oranges with Padded Straight Stitches (Straight Stitch over Colonial Knot) using two colors. Fill in between oranges with Colonial Knots. Add Ribbon Stitch leaves around oranges.

Wreath

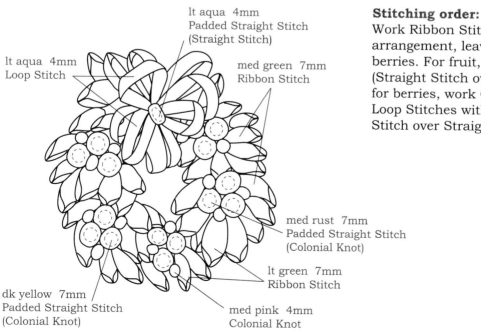

lt aqua 4mm
Padded Straight Stitch
(Straight Stitch)

lt aqua 4mm
Loop Stitch

med green 7mm
Ribbon Stitch

med rust 7mm
Padded Straight Stitch
(Colonial Knot)

lt green 7mm
Ribbon Stitch

med pink 4mm
Colonial Knot

dk yellow 7mm
Padded Straight Stitch
(Colonial Knot)

Stitching order:
Work Ribbon Stitch leaves in random color arrangement, leaving spaces to work fruit and berries. For fruit, work Padded Straight Stitches (Straight Stitch over Colonial Knot) in two colors; for berries, work Colonial Knots. For bow, work Loop Stitches with Padded Straight Stitch (Straight Stitch over Straight Stitch) at center.

Country Bouquet

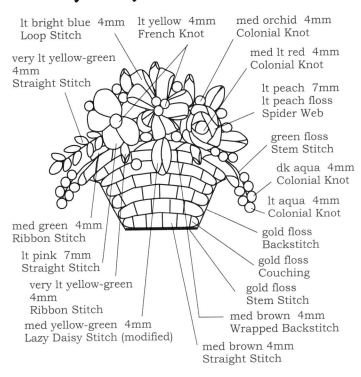

lt bright blue 4mm
Loop Stitch

lt yellow 4mm
French Knot

med orchid 4mm
Colonial Knot

med lt red 4mm
Colonial Knot

very lt yellow-green
4mm
Straight Stitch

lt peach 7mm
lt peach floss
Spider Web

green floss
Stem Stitch

dk aqua 4mm
Colonial Knot

lt aqua 4mm
Colonial Knot

gold floss
Backstitch

gold floss
Couching

gold floss
Stem Stitch

med green 4mm
Ribbon Stitch

lt pink 7mm
Straight Stitch

very lt yellow-green
4mm
Ribbon Stitch

med yellow-green 4mm
Lazy Daisy Stitch (modified)

med brown 4mm
Wrapped Backstitch

med brown 4mm
Straight Stitch

Stitching order:

To make side of basket, start at the bottom and work closely spaced, loose Straight Stitches. Couch each Straight Stitch with floss, working vertical stitches in an alternating design to simulate weaving; increase the curve as you move upward. For rim, work Wrapped Backstitch. Use floss to Backstitch sides and Stem Stitch bottom.

Extending down from each side, use floss to Stem Stitch stems; work ribbon Colonial Knots along each side. On left side, work another downward stem with floss, adding Straight Stitch leaves along each side. At center front and right side above rim, work three modified Lazy Daisy leaves. Across rim, work Ribbon Stitch leaves overlapping edge, with some extending upward at center.

Work left flower with five loose Straight Stitches and a French Knot at center. Work middle flower with eight Loop Stitches and a cluster of three French Knots at center. For third flower, work a Spider Web Rose with a Colonial Knot at center. Above flowers, work more Ribbon Stitch leaves, tucking some beneath flowers. Work Colonial Knots scattered around bouquet and on basket.

Mom

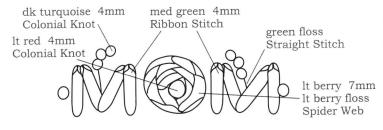

dk turquoise 4mm
Colonial Knot

lt red 4mm
Colonial Knot

med green 4mm
Ribbon Stitch

green floss
Straight Stitch

lt berry 7mm
lt berry floss
Spider Web

Stitching order:

Work a Spider Web Rose, filling in center with a Colonial Knot. On each side of rose, work Ribbon Stitch letters. Straight Stitch the stems and add Colonial Knots.

Tulip Bouquet

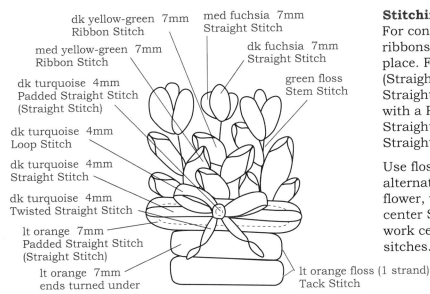

dk yellow-green 7mm
Ribbon Stitch

med fuchsia 7mm
Straight Stitch

med yellow-green 7mm
Ribbon Stitch

dk fuchsia 7mm
Straight Stitch

dk turquoise 4mm
Padded Straight Stitch
(Straight Stitch)

green floss
Stem Stitch

dk turquoise 4mm
Loop Stitch

dk turquoise 4mm
Straight Stitch

dk turquoise 4mm
Twisted Straight Stitch

lt orange 7mm
Padded Straight Stitch
(Straight Stitch)

lt orange 7mm
ends turned under

lt orange floss (1 strand)
Tack Stitch

Stitching order:

For container, cut two pieces of ribbon. Place ribbons horizontally and pin ends under; tack in place. For rim, work a Padded Straight Stitch (Straight Stitch over Straight Stitch), topped with a Straight Stitch. For bow, work two Loop Stitches with a Padded Straight Stitch (Straight Stitch over Straight Stitch) at center. Work two Twisted Straight Stitches for streamers.

Use floss to Stem Stitch stems. Work leaves in alternating colors of Ribbon Stitches. For center flower, work two side Straight Stitches with a center Straight Stitch on top. On each side flower, work center stitch first, then overlap the side sitches.

35

Father's Day

Fishing Pole

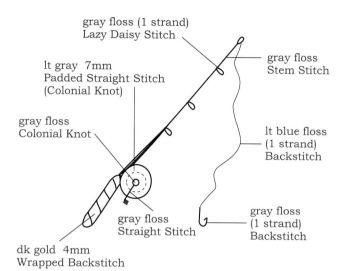

gray floss (1 strand)
Lazy Daisy Stitch

lt gray 7mm
Padded Straight Stitch
(Colonial Knot)

gray floss
Colonial Knot

gray floss
Stem Stitch

lt blue floss
(1 strand)
Backstitch

gray floss
Straight Stitch

gray floss
(1 strand)
Backstitch

dk gold 4mm
Wrapped Backstitch

Stitching order:
For handle, work Wrapped Backstitch; use floss to work Stem Stitches for rod, beginning with two rows and tapering to one row. Work Lazy Daisies along lower edge and end of rod. For the reel, work a Padded Straight Stitch (Straight Stitch over Colonial Knot) topped with a Colonial Knot and Straight Stitches in floss. Use floss to Backstitch line; add a Backstitch hook at end.

Fish

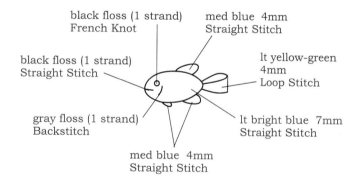

black floss (1 strand)
French Knot

med blue 4mm
Straight Stitch

black floss (1 strand)
Straight Stitch

lt yellow-green
4mm
Loop Stitch

gray floss (1 strand)
Backstitch

lt bright blue 7mm
Straight Stitch

med blue 4mm
Straight Stitch

Stitching order:
Work a Straight Stitch for body and a Loop Stitch for tail. For upper and lower fins, work three Straight Stitches, starting each one beneath edges of body. Use floss to work a French Knot for eye, a Straight Stitch for mouth, and Backstitch the gill.

Fish Decoy

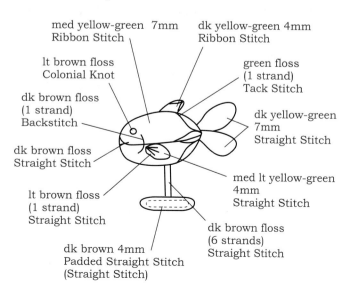

med yellow-green 7mm
Ribbon Stitch

dk yellow-green 4mm
Ribbon Stitch

lt brown floss
Colonial Knot

green floss
(1 strand)
Tack Stitch

dk brown floss
(1 strand)
Backstitch

dk yellow-green
7mm
Straight Stitch

dk brown floss
Straight Stitch

lt brown floss
(1 strand)
Straight Stitch

med lt yellow-green
4mm
Straight Stitch

dk brown floss
(6 strands)
Straight Stitch

dk brown 4mm
Padded Straight Stitch
(Straight Stitch)

Stitching order:
Work two Ribbon Stitches for body, two Straight Stitches for tail, and a Ribbon Stitch for upper fin, tacking with floss to retain shape. For the side fin, work a Straight Stitch, topped with floss Straight Stitches. Use floss to Backstitch the gill, work a Colonial Knot for eye, and a Straight Stitch for mouth. For the base, use floss to work two vertical Straight Stitches; work a horizontal Padded Straight Stitch (Straight Stitch over Straight Stitch) slightly overlapping vertical stitches.

Fishing Flies

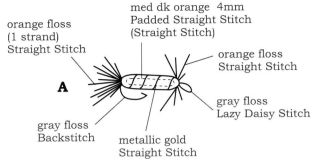

orange floss
(1 strand)
Straight Stitch

med dk orange 4mm
Padded Straight Stitch
(Straight Stitch)

orange floss
Straight Stitch

A

gray floss
Lazy Daisy Stitch

gray floss
Backstitch

metallic gold
Straight Stitch

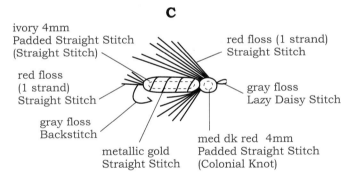

B

green floss (1 strand)
Stem Stitch

black 4mm
Padded Straight Stitch
(Colonial Knot)

green floss
(1 strand)
Straight Stitch

gray floss
Lazy Daisy Stitch

gray floss
Backstitch

med yellow 4mm
Padded Straight Stitch
(Straight Stitch)

metallic gold
Straight Stitch

C

ivory 4mm
Padded Straight Stitch
(Straight Stitch)

red floss (1 strand)
Straight Stitch

red floss
(1 strand)
Straight Stitch

gray floss
Lazy Daisy Stitch

gray floss
Backstitch

metallic gold
Straight Stitch

med dk red 4mm
Padded Straight Stitch
(Colonial Knot)

Stitching order:
Version A
Work body with a Padded Straight Stitch (Straight Stitch over Straight Stitch); work Straight Stitch diagonal lines across body. Use floss to work a Lazy Daisy at right end with Straight Stitches above and below joining. Using floss, work Straight Stitches at opposite end and Backstitch the hook.

Version B
Work body with a Padded Straight Stitch (Straight Stitch over Straight Stitch); work Straight Stitch diagonal lines across body. Work a Padded Straight Stitch (Straight Stitch over Colonial Knot) for head; using floss, work a Lazy Daisy extending from head. Use floss to work three groups of Straight Stitches with a Stem Stitch spine along center of large group. Backstitch the hook.

Version C
Work body with a Padded Straight Stitch (Straight Stitch over Straight Stitch); work Straight Stitch diagonal lines across body. Work a Padded Straight Stitch (Straight Stitch over Colonial Knot) for head; using floss, work a Lazy Daisy extending from head. Use floss to work three groups of Straight Stitches and Backstitch the hook.

Mallard Duck

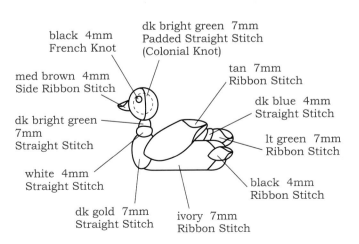

black 4mm
French Knot

dk bright green 7mm
Padded Straight Stitch
(Colonial Knot)

med brown 4mm
Side Ribbon Stitch

tan 7mm
Ribbon Stitch

dk bright green
7mm
Straight Stitch

dk blue 4mm
Straight Stitch

lt green 7mm
Ribbon Stitch

white 4mm
Straight Stitch

black 4mm
Ribbon Stitch

dk gold 7mm
Straight Stitch

ivory 7mm
Ribbon Stitch

Stitching order:
For upper back, work a short Ribbon Stitch with two overlapping Straight Stitches on left end. For lower back, work a Ribbon Stitch, slightly covering lower edge of upper back, and a Ribbon Stitch at right end for tail. Work a Straight Stitch for breast, Ribbon Stitch for wing, a tightly pulled Straight Stitch for upper neck, and a Straight Stitch for lower neck. For the head, work two Padded Straight Stitches (Straight Stitch over Colonial Knot) topped with a French Knot for eye; work a Side Ribbon Stitch for beak.

Golf Club and Ball

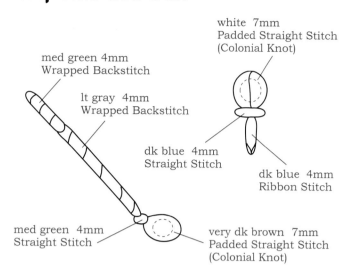

med green 4mm
Wrapped Backstitch

lt gray 4mm
Wrapped Backstitch

white 7mm
Padded Straight Stitch
(Colonial Knot)

dk blue 4mm
Straight Stitch

dk blue 4mm
Ribbon Stitch

med green 4mm
Straight Stitch

very dk brown 7mm
Padded Straight Stitch
(Colonial Knot)

Stitching order:

For club head, work a Padded Straight Stitch (Straight Stitch over Colonial Knot). At base of club, work a small Straight Stitch; then, moving upwards, work Wrapped Backstitch in two colors.

For ball, work Padded Straight Stitch (two Straight Stitches over a Colonial Knot). For tee, work a vertical Ribbon Stitch, with a horizontal Straight Stitch covering top point.

Tennis Racket and Ball

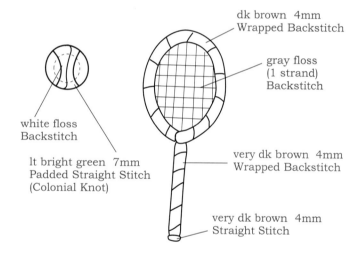

dk brown 4mm
Wrapped Backstitch

gray floss
(1 strand)
Backstitch

white floss
Backstitch

lt bright green 7mm
Padded Straight Stitch
(Colonial Knot)

very dk brown 4mm
Wrapped Backstitch

very dk brown 4mm
Straight Stitch

Stitching order:

For ball, work Padded Straight Stitch (two Straight Stitches over a Colonial Knot); use floss to Backstitch lines on ball.

For rim of racket, work Wrapped Backstitch in an oval, beginning and ending at the bottom. For handle, work Wrapped Backstitch, then work a short horizontal Straight Stitch at bottom. Use floss to Backstitch vertical and horizontal strings.

Baseball and Bat

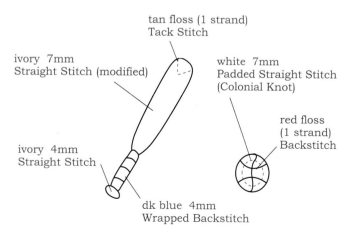

tan floss (1 strand)
Tack Stitch

ivory 7mm
Straight Stitch (modified)

white 7mm
Padded Straight Stitch
(Colonial Knot)

red floss
(1 strand)
Backstitch

ivory 4mm
Straight Stitch

dk blue 4mm
Wrapped Backstitch

Stitching order:

For bat, work a modified Straight Stitch. For handle, work Wrapped Backstitch with a short horizontal Straight Stitch at bottom.

For ball, work Padded Straight Stitch (two Straight Stitches over a Colonial Knot); use floss to Backstitch lines on ball.

Graduation

Diploma

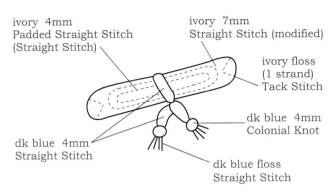

ivory 4mm
Padded Straight Stitch
(Straight Stitch)

ivory 7mm
Straight Stitch (modified)

ivory floss
(1 strand)
Tack Stitch

dk blue 4mm
Colonial Knot

dk blue 4mm
Straight Stitch

dk blue floss
Straight Stitch

Stitching order:
Work a Padded Straight Stitch (Straight Stitch over two Straight Stitches) covered with a modified Straight Stitch. Tack both ends under; tack sides as needed. At center, work a Straight Stitch, with two Straight Stitches for streamers. Work a Colonial Knot at each end, and use floss to work Straight Stitch tassel ends.

Mortarboard

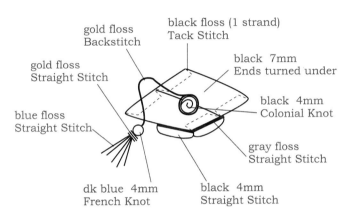

gold floss
Backstitch

black floss (1 strand)
Tack Stitch

gold floss
Straight Stitch

black 7mm
Ends turned under

blue floss
Straight Stitch

black 4mm
Colonial Knot

gray floss
Straight Stitch

dk blue 4mm
French Knot

black 4mm
Straight Stitch

Note: Work tassel to match school color(s).
Stitching order:
Cut two pieces of ribbon. Place ribbons horizontally and pin ends under diagonally to create board shape; tack in place. Below lowest corner, work two Straight Stitches; use floss to top each with a Straight Stitch. At center of board work a Colonial Knot; use floss to encircle knot and Backstitch the cord. At end of cord, work a French Knot; use floss to work three short horizontal Straight Stitches and tassel ends.

Award Cup

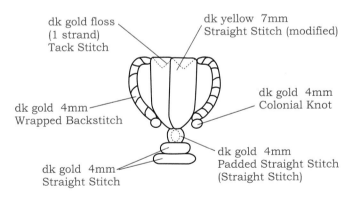

dk gold floss
(1 strand)
Tack Stitch

dk yellow 7mm
Straight Stitch (modified)

dk gold 4mm
Wrapped Backstitch

dk gold 4mm
Colonial Knot

dk gold 4mm
Straight Stitch

dk gold 4mm
Padded Straight Stitch
(Straight Stitch)

Stitching order:
For cup, work two modified Straight Stitches. For handles, work Wrapped Backstitch on each side with a Colonial Knot at bottom. For the base, work a vertical Padded Straight Stitch (Straight Stitch over Straight Stitch) and two horizontal Straight Stitches, the lower one slightly wider.

Key

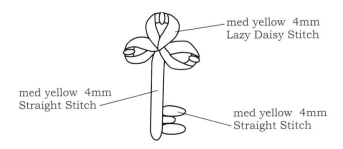

med yellow 4mm
Lazy Daisy Stitch

med yellow 4mm
Straight Stitch

med yellow 4mm
Straight Stitch

Stitching order:
Work a long vertical Straight Stitch; at lower end, work three horizontal Straight Stitches. At top of key, work three Lazy Daisies.

Wedding & Anniversary

Wedding Bells

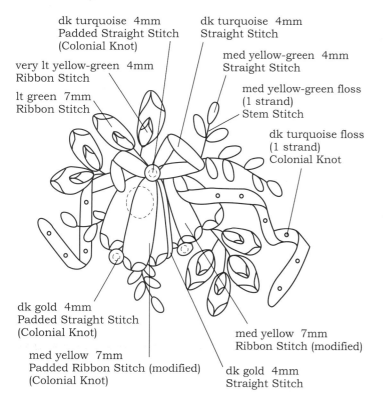

dk turquoise 4mm
Padded Straight Stitch
(Colonial Knot)

dk turquoise 4mm
Straight Stitch

very lt yellow-green 4mm
Ribbon Stitch

med yellow-green 4mm
Straight Stitch

lt green 7mm
Ribbon Stitch

med yellow-green floss
(1 strand)
Stem Stitch

dk turquoise floss
(1 strand)
Colonial Knot

dk gold 4mm
Padded Straight Stitch
(Colonial Knot)

med yellow 7mm
Padded Ribbon Stitch (modified)
(Colonial Knot)

dk gold 4mm
Straight Stitch

med yellow 7mm
Ribbon Stitch (modified)

Stitching order:

For right bell, work three modified Ribbon Stitches. For left bell, work a Straight Stitch, then three modified Padded Ribbon Stitches (Straight Stitch over Colonial Knot). Work a Padded Straight Stitch (Straight Stitch over Colonial Knot) for clapper on each bell.

For bow, work five Straight Stitches at top of bells, with a Padded Straight Stitch (Straight Stitch over Colonial Knot) at center. For streamers, work a long Straight Stitch, twisting and turning in a pleasing design; Couch down with Colonial Knots. For large leaves, work Ribbon Stitch topped with a smaller Ribbon Stitch. For remaining leaves, work Straight Stitches. Work all stems with floss Stem Stitch.

Intertwined Rings

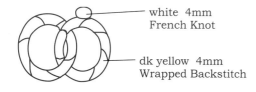

white 4mm
French Knot

dk yellow 4mm
Wrapped Backstitch

Stitching order:

Work two Wrapped Backstitch rings overlapping at center. Work a French Knot on top of right ring.

Wedding Cake

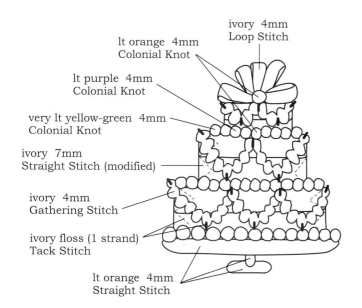

ivory 4mm
Loop Stitch

lt orange 4mm
Colonial Knot

lt purple 4mm
Colonial Knot

very lt yellow-green 4mm
Colonial Knot

ivory 7mm
Straight Stitch (modified)

ivory 4mm
Gathering Stitch

ivory floss (1 strand)
Tack Stitch

lt orange 4mm
Straight Stitch

Stitching order:

For cake plate, work a short horizontal Straight Stitch for base, overlapped with a vertical Straight Stitch; add a long horizontal Straight Stitch covering top of vertical stitch.

For cake, work horizontal modified Straight Stitches, to create three layers. On each layer, work Gathering Stitch, tacking at top and bottom of zigzag rows. At base of cake, and between remaining two layers, work Colonial Knots in a random color arrangement. On top of cake, work five Loop Stitches with a Colonial Knot at center.

Anniversary

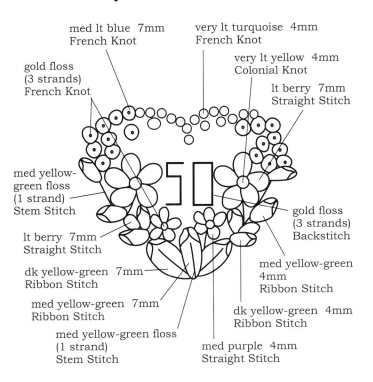

med lt blue 7mm
French Knot

very lt turquoise 4mm
French Knot

gold floss
(3 strands)
French Knot

very lt yellow 4mm
Colonial Knot

lt berry 7mm
Straight Stitch

med yellow-
green floss
(1 strand)
Stem Stitch

gold floss
(3 strands)
Backstitch

lt berry 7mm
Straight Stitch

dk yellow-green 7mm
Ribbon Stitch

med yellow-green
4mm
Ribbon Stitch

med yellow-green 7mm
Ribbon Stitch

dk yellow-green 4mm
Ribbon Stitch

med yellow-green floss
(1 strand)
Stem Stitch

med purple 4mm
Straight Stitch

Stitching order:

Stem Stitch a heart shape for base of design. Beginning at bottom of heart, work two Ribbon Stitch leaves, topped with a vertical Ribbon Stitch leaf. On each side of leaf, work flowers with five Straight Stitches and a floss French Knot at center. Continuing up heart outline, work alternating colors of Ribbon Stitch leaves; add a Straight Stitch bud in center of each pair of lower leaves. For larger flowers, work five loose Straight Stitches with a Colonial Knot at center. Work loose French Knots, topped with floss French Knots, then plain French Knots, becoming tighter towards top. Work Stem Stitches for flower stems and leaf veins. Using the numerals below, trace or lightly draw desired number and use floss to Backstitch in place.

1234567890

Anniversary Bouquet

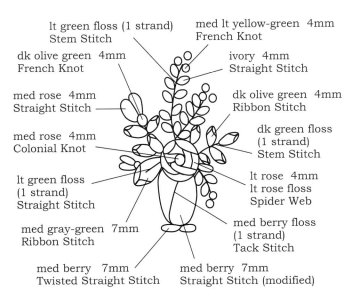

lt green floss (1 strand)
Stem Stitch

med lt yellow-green 4mm
French Knot

dk olive green 4mm
French Knot

ivory 4mm
Straight Stitch

med rose 4mm
Straight Stitch

dk olive green 4mm
Ribbon Stitch

med rose 4mm
Colonial Knot

dk green floss
(1 strand)
Stem Stitch

lt green floss
(1 strand)
Straight Stitch

lt rose 4mm
lt rose floss
Spider Web

med gray-green 7mm
Ribbon Stitch

med berry floss
(1 strand)
Tack Stitch

med berry 7mm
Twisted Straight Stitch

med berry 7mm
Straight Stitch (modified)

Stitching order:

Work base of vase with a horizontal Twisted Straight Stitch, then two modified Straight Stitches for vase. Work a Spider Web rose at top center of vase, overlapping top edge; work Colonial Knot at center. Work a Ribbon Stitch leaf at lower left of rose; use floss to work leaf vein with Straight Stitch and stems with Stem Stitch. On left side, work two Straight Stitch buds, each with a French Knot at bottom. Work Ribbon Stitch leaves on each side of some stems; then work Straight Stitch leaves for remaining stems, ending with French Knots.

Bridal Bouquet

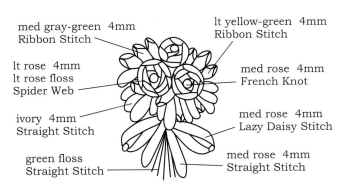

med gray-green 4mm
Ribbon Stitch

lt yellow-green 4mm
Ribbon Stitch

lt rose 4mm
lt rose floss
Spider Web

med rose 4mm
French Knot

ivory 4mm
Straight Stitch

med rose 4mm
Lazy Daisy Stitch

green floss
Straight Stitch

med rose 4mm
Straight Stitch

Stitching order:

For the stems, work floss Straight Stitches overlapping at top, and spreading out at bottom. Work a Lazy Daisy and a Straight Stitch on each side of stems. Work crescent-shaped base with Straight Stitches. Work three Spider Web Roses; for the topmost rose, have center of spokes toward top of blossom. Add a French Knot to each rose. Fill in around roses with the two shades of Ribbon Stitch leaves.

Fourth of July

Flags

A

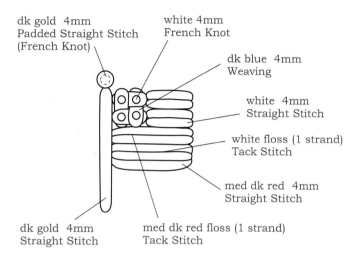

dk gold 4mm
Padded Straight Stitch
(French Knot)

white 4mm
French Knot

dk blue 4mm
Weaving

white 4mm
Straight Stitch

white floss (1 strand)
Tack Stitch

med dk red 4mm
Straight Stitch

dk gold 4mm
Straight Stitch

med dk red floss (1 strand)
Tack Stitch

Stitching order:
Version A
Work Straight Stitch for flagpole, and Padded
Straight Stitch (Straight Stitch over French Knot)
for knob. Weave upper left corner of flag; add four
French Knots. Work remaining flag with pairs of
Straight Stitches, tacking as needed to keep stripes
straight.

B

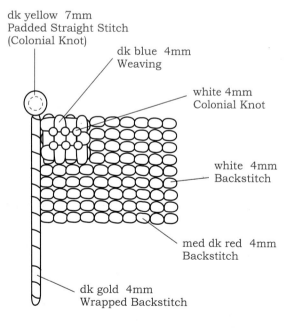

dk yellow 7mm
Padded Straight Stitch
(Colonial Knot)

dk blue 4mm
Weaving

white 4mm
Colonial Knot

white 4mm
Backstitch

med dk red 4mm
Backstitch

dk gold 4mm
Wrapped Backstitch

Version B
Work Wrapped Backstitch for flagpole and Padded
Straight Stitch (Straight Stitch over Colonial Knot)
for knob. Weave upper left corner of flag; work
Colonial Knots at edges of intersections. Work
remaining flag with Backstitch.

Patriotic Heart

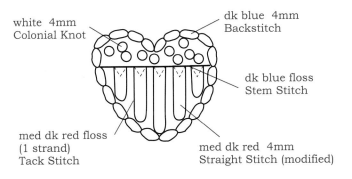

white 4mm
Colonial Knot

dk blue 4mm
Backstitch

dk blue floss
Stem Stitch

med dk red floss
(1 strand)
Tack Stitch

med dk red 4mm
Straight Stitch (modified)

Stitching order:
Work Backstitch in shape of a heart. On top third of heart work Colonial Knots; use floss to Stem Stitch a horizontal line below knots. Work five vertical modified Straight Stitches of various lengths below horizontal line.

Firecrackers

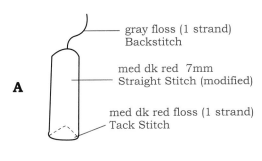

gray floss (1 strand)
Backstitch

med dk red 7mm
Straight Stitch (modified)

med dk red floss (1 strand)
Tack Stitch

A

Stitching order:
Version A
Work a modified Straight Stitch, tacking on each side at bottom and top. Work Backstitch for fuse.

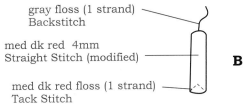

gray floss (1 strand)
Backstitch

med dk red 4mm
Straight Stitch (modified)

med dk red floss (1 strand)
Tack Stitch

B

Version B
Work same as Version A.

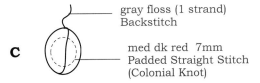

gray floss (1 strand)
Backstitch

med dk red 7mm
Padded Straight Stitch
(Colonial Knot)

C

Version C
Work Padded Straight Stitch (two Straight Stitches over a Colonial Knot); work Backstitch for fuse.

Ribbon Award

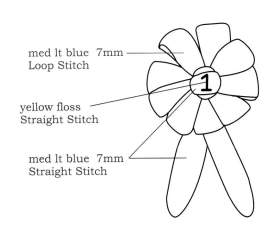

med lt blue 7mm
Loop Stitch

yellow floss
Straight Stitch

med lt blue 7mm
Straight Stitch

Stitching order:
Work nine Loop Stitches; cover center with two Straight Stitches. Use floss to work Straight Stitches for number. Work two overlapping Straight Stitches for streamers, beginning under edges of Loop Stitches.

Birthday

Birthday Cakes

A

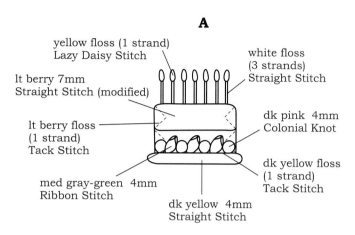

yellow floss (1 strand)
Lazy Daisy Stitch

white floss
(3 strands)
Straight Stitch

lt berry 7mm
Straight Stitch (modified)

lt berry floss
(1 strand)
Tack Stitch

dk pink 4mm
Colonial Knot

dk yellow floss
(1 strand)
Tack Stitch

med gray-green 4mm
Ribbon Stitch

dk yellow 4mm
Straight Stitch

B

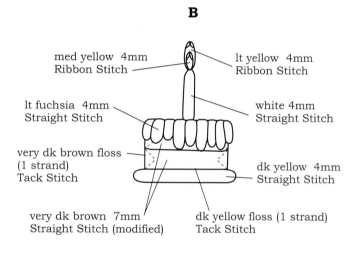

med yellow 4mm
Ribbon Stitch

lt yellow 4mm
Ribbon Stitch

lt fuchsia 4mm
Straight Stitch

white 4mm
Straight Stitch

very dk brown floss
(1 strand)
Tack Stitch

dk yellow 4mm
Straight Stitch

very dk brown 7mm
Straight Stitch (modified)

dk yellow floss (1 strand)
Tack Stitch

Stitching order:
Version A
Work two horizontal modified Straight Stitches for cake, tacking ends and edges in place. Work a Straight Stitch for plate, tacking down to lower edge of plate. Work Colonial Knots for roses and Ribbon Stitches for leaves at base of cake. Use floss to work Straight Stitches for candles, topped with Lazy Daisies for flames.

Version B
Work two horizontal modified Straight Stitches for cake, tacking ends and edges in place. Work a Straight Stitch for plate, tacking down to lower edge of cake. For frosting, work various lengths of Straight Stitches. Work candle with Straight Stitch; add one Ribbon Stitch topped with a smaller Ribbon Stitch for flame.

Birthday Bouquet

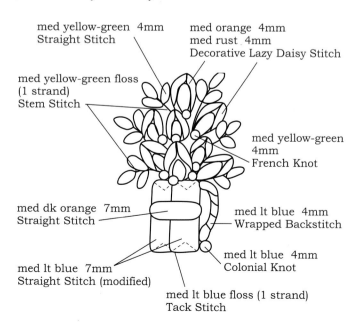

med yellow-green 4mm
Straight Stitch

med orange 4mm
med rust 4mm
Decorative Lazy Daisy Stitch

med yellow-green floss
(1 strand)
Stem Stitch

med yellow-green
4mm
French Knot

med dk orange 7mm
Straight Stitch

med lt blue 4mm
Wrapped Backstitch

med lt blue 4mm
Colonial Knot

med lt blue 7mm
Straight Stitch (modified)

med lt blue floss (1 strand)
Tack Stitch

Stitching order:
Work two vertical modified Straight Stitches tacked at bottom and top for pitcher; add a horizontal Straight Stitch across center. For handle, work Wrapped Backstitch beginning slightly below top and ending slightly above bottom; work a Colonial Knot at bottom. For each flower, work a Decorative Lazy Daisy; add a French Knot at bottom. Fill in with Straight Stitch leaves. Use floss to Stem Stitch stems.

Ice Cream Cone

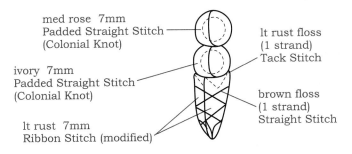

med rose 7mm
Padded Straight Stitch
(Colonial Knot)

lt rust floss
(1 strand)
Tack Stitch

ivory 7mm
Padded Straight Stitch
(Colonial Knot)

brown floss
(1 strand)
Straight Stitch

lt rust 7mm
Ribbon Stitch (modified)

Stitching order:
Work two overlapping modified Ribbon Stitches for cone then add Straight Stitch crosshatching. Tack as needed to retain shape. Work two Padded Straight Stitches (Straight Stitch over Colonial Knot), one above the other, for ice cream.

Pink Candy

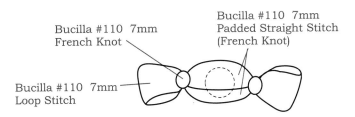

Bucilla #110 7mm
French Knot

Bucilla #110 7mm
Padded Straight Stitch
(French Knot)

Bucilla #110 7mm
Loop Stitch

Stitching order:
Work Padded Straight Stitch (two Straight Stitches over a French Knot) for center of candy; add a Loop Stitch at each end, topped with a French Knot.
Note: Use organza as shown or any other desired ribbon.

Balloons

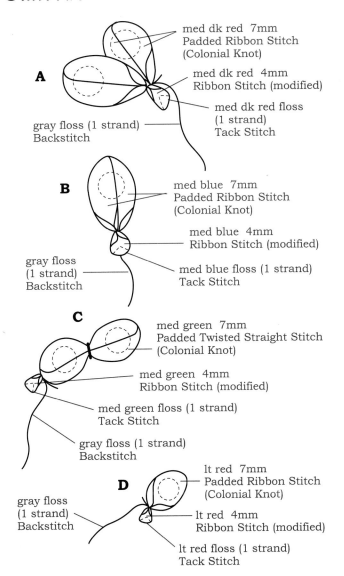

A

med dk red 7mm
Padded Ribbon Stitch
(Colonial Knot)

med dk red 4mm
Ribbon Stitch (modified)

med dk red floss
(1 strand)
Tack Stitch

gray floss (1 strand)
Backstitch

B

med blue 7mm
Padded Ribbon Stitch
(Colonial Knot)

med blue 4mm
Ribbon Stitch (modified)

med blue floss (1 strand)
Tack Stitch

gray floss
(1 strand)
Backstitch

C

med green 7mm
Padded Twisted Straight Stitch
(Colonial Knot)

med green 4mm
Ribbon Stitch (modified)

med green floss (1 strand)
Tack Stitch

gray floss (1 strand)
Backstitch

D

lt red 7mm
Padded Ribbon Stitch
(Colonial Knot)

lt red 4mm
Ribbon Stitch (modified)

lt red floss (1 strand)
Tack Stitch

gray floss
(1 strand)
Backstitch

Stitching order:
Version A
For each balloon, work Padded Ribbon Stitch (two Ribbon Stitches over a Colonial Knot) with bottoms overlapping; tack as needed to cover knot and retain shape. Work a modified Ribbon Stitch at bottom of balloons, then use floss to Backstitch string.

Version B
Work Padded Ribbon Stitch (two Ribbon Stitches over a Colonial Knot); tack as needed to cover knot and retain shape. Work a modified Ribbon Stitch at bottom. Use floss to Backstitch string.

Version C
For the twisted balloon, insert two pieces of ribbon into needle and treat them as one. Work a Padded Twisted Straight Stitch (Twisted Straight Stitch over two Colonial Knots), tacking at center and as needed to retain shape. Work a modified Ribbon Stitch at bottom; use floss to Backstitch string.

Version D
Work same as Version B, making a smaller stitch.

Halloween

Bats

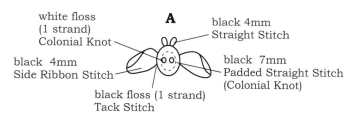

white floss
(1 strand)
Colonial Knot

black 4mm
Side Ribbon Stitch

A

black 4mm
Straight Stitch

black 7mm
Padded Straight Stitch
(Colonial Knot)

black floss (1 strand)
Tack Stitch

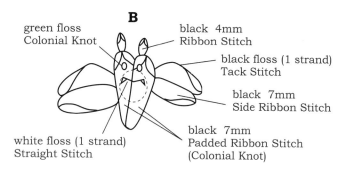

B

green floss
Colonial Knot

black 4mm
Ribbon Stitch

black floss (1 strand)
Tack Stitch

black 7mm
Side Ribbon Stitch

white floss (1 strand)
Straight Stitch

black 7mm
Padded Ribbon Stitch
(Colonial Knot)

Stitching order:

Version A

For body, work Padded Straight Stitch (Straight Stitch over Colonial Knot). Work Straight Stitches for ears. Use floss for Colonial Knot eyes. For each wing, work a Side Ribbon Stitch; tack with floss to retain shape.

Version B

For body, work Padded Ribbon Stitch (two Ribbon Stitches over a Colonial Knot); use floss for Colonial Knot eyes. For mouth and teeth, use floss to work two short Straight Stitches angled from center; at each end, work three Straight Stitches to form a pointed tooth. For ears, work two Ribbon Stitches. For each wing, work two Side Ribbon Stitches; tack with floss to retain shape.

Boo

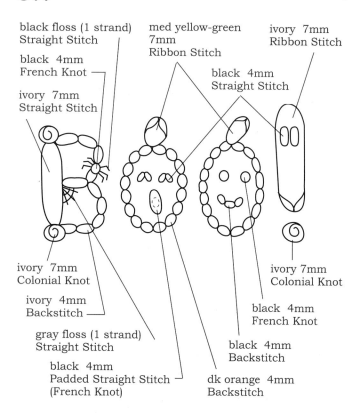

black floss (1 strand)
Straight Stitch

black 4mm
French Knot

ivory 7mm
Straight Stitch

med yellow-green
7mm
Ribbon Stitch

ivory 7mm
Ribbon Stitch

black 4mm
Straight Stitch

ivory 7mm
Colonial Knot

ivory 4mm
Backstitch

gray floss (1 strand)
Straight Stitch

black 4mm
Padded Straight Stitch
(French Knot)

dk orange 4mm
Backstitch

black 4mm
Backstitch

black 4mm
French Knot

ivory 7mm
Colonial Knot

Stitching order:

For "B," work a vertical Straight Stitch with Colonial Knots at top and bottom. For remainder of letter, work Backstitches to form shape. Work a French Knot for spider body. Use floss to Straight Stitch legs and web. For the two "Os," work Backstitches in an oval shape, with a Ribbon Stitch on top for stem. Inside left "O," work two pairs of Straight Stitches for eyes and a Padded Straight Stitch (Straight Stitch over French Knot) for mouth. Inside right "O," work two French Knots for eyes and Backstitches for mouth. For the exclamation point, work a vertical Ribbon Stitch and a Colonial Knot, with two Straight Stitches for eyes.

Spider

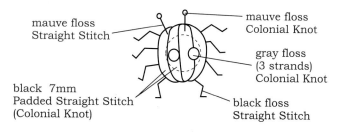

mauve floss
Straight Stitch

mauve floss
Colonial Knot

gray floss
(3 strands)
Colonial Knot

black 7mm
Padded Straight Stitch
(Colonial Knot)

black floss
Straight Stitch

Stitching order:

Work Padded Straight Stitch (four Straight Stitches over a Colonial Knot). Use floss to Straight Stitch two antennae with a Colonial Knot at each end; work Colonial Knots for eyes and Straight Stitches for legs.

Jack-O'-Lanterns

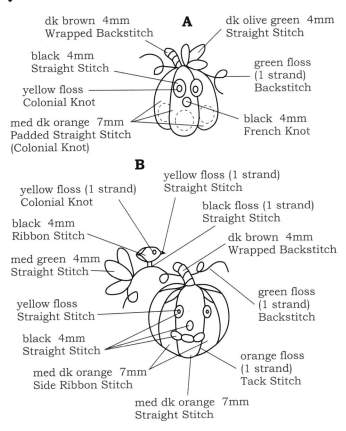

A

dk brown 4mm Wrapped Backstitch

black 4mm Straight Stitch

yellow floss Colonial Knot

med dk orange 7mm Padded Straight Stitch (Colonial Knot)

dk olive green 4mm Straight Stitch

green floss (1 strand) Backstitch

black 4mm French Knot

B

yellow floss (1 strand) Colonial Knot

black 4mm Ribbon Stitch

med green 4mm Straight Stitch

yellow floss Straight Stitch

black 4mm Straight Stitch

med dk orange 7mm Side Ribbon Stitch

yellow floss (1 strand) Straight Stitch

black floss (1 strand) Straight Stitch

dk brown 4mm Wrapped Backstitch

green floss (1 strand) Backstitch

orange floss (1 strand) Tack Stitch

med dk orange 7mm Straight Stitch

Stitching order:

Version A

For pumpkin, work three Padded Straight Stitches (Straight Stitch over Colonial Knot), with the center one on top. For each eye, work a Straight Stitch topped with a floss Colonial Knot. Work a French Knot for nose, Wrapped Backstitch for stem, and three Straight Stitches for leaves. Use floss to Backstitch tendrils.

Version B

For pumpkin, work four Side Ribbon Stitches (two on each side); work a Straight Stitch over the center. Tack with floss to retain shape. For each eye, work a Straight Stitch topped with a floss Straight Stitch. For nose and mouth, work Straight Stitches; add a Wrapped Backstitch for stem. Use floss to Backstitch tendrils. For leaves, work three Straight Stitches with center one on top. To make raven, work a horizontal Ribbon Stitch; use floss for the Colonial Knot eye and Straight Stitches for beak and feet.

Black Cat

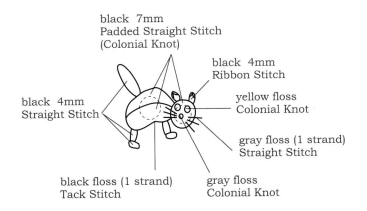

black 7mm Padded Straight Stitch (Colonial Knot)

black 4mm Straight Stitch

black 4mm Ribbon Stitch

yellow floss Colonial Knot

gray floss (1 strand) Straight Stitch

black floss (1 strand) Tack Stitch

gray floss Colonial Knot

Stitching order:

To make body, work Padded Straight Stitch (two Straight Stitches over a Colonial Knot), using floss to tack body into desired shape. For head, work a Padded Straight Stitch (Straight Stitch over Colonial Knot) and use floss to tack head to body. Use floss to work Colonial Knot eyes and nose and Straight Stitch whiskers. For ears, work two Ribbon Stitches. Work Straight Stitches for tail, legs, and paws.

Guess Who!

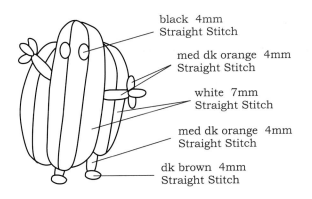

black 4mm Straight Stitch

med dk orange 4mm Straight Stitch

white 7mm Straight Stitch

med dk orange 4mm Straight Stitch

dk brown 4mm Straight Stitch

Stitching order:

For body, work two pairs of Straight Stitches with three more Straight Stitches centered on top. Add two Straight Stitches for eyes. For each arm, work a Straight Stitch with three Straight Stitches at end. For each leg, work a Straight Stitch with another Straight Stitch at an angle.

Judaic

7 Species with Hai (Life)

Stitching order:

Starting at the top, work the date palm with a Wrapped Backstitch trunk, topped with Ribbon Stitches for leaves; work French Knots for fruit and use floss to Backstitch stems. Moving clockwise, make fig by using floss to Stem Stitch the stems. Work ripe (red) fruit with a Padded Ribbon Stitch (Ribbon Stitch over Colonial Knot), unripe fruit with a Padded Ribbon Stitch (Ribbon Stitch over French Knot), and bud with a Padded Straight Stitch (Straight Stitch over Straight Stitch).

Work each leaf cluster with five Ribbon Stitches, making the middle one longer and on top.

Make the wheat by using floss to Stem Stitch a stem; work two rows of Padded Ribbon Stitches (Ribbon Stitch over French Knot), beginning with a single stitch at the top. Use floss to work Straight Stitches at ends. Add one long Twisted Ribbon Stitch, tacking to hold shape.

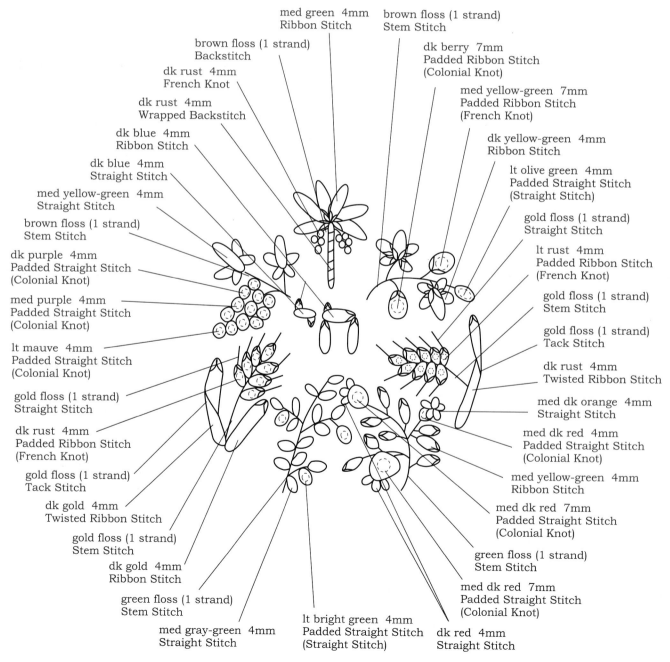

med green 4mm
Ribbon Stitch

brown floss (1 strand)
Stem Stitch

brown floss (1 strand)
Backstitch

dk berry 7mm
Padded Ribbon Stitch
(Colonial Knot)

dk rust 4mm
French Knot

dk rust 4mm
Wrapped Backstitch

med yellow-green 7mm
Padded Ribbon Stitch
(French Knot)

dk blue 4mm
Ribbon Stitch

dk yellow-green 4mm
Ribbon Stitch

dk blue 4mm
Straight Stitch

lt olive green 4mm
Padded Straight Stitch
(Straight Stitch)

med yellow-green 4mm
Straight Stitch

gold floss (1 strand)
Straight Stitch

brown floss (1 strand)
Stem Stitch

lt rust 4mm
Padded Ribbon Stitch
(French Knot)

dk purple 4mm
Padded Straight Stitch
(Colonial Knot)

gold floss (1 strand)
Stem Stitch

med purple 4mm
Padded Straight Stitch
(Colonial Knot)

gold floss (1 strand)
Tack Stitch

lt mauve 4mm
Padded Straight Stitch
(Colonial Knot)

dk rust 4mm
Twisted Ribbon Stitch

gold floss (1 strand)
Straight Stitch

med dk orange 4mm
Straight Stitch

dk rust 4mm
Padded Ribbon Stitch
(French Knot)

med dk red 4mm
Padded Straight Stitch
(Colonial Knot)

gold floss (1 strand)
Tack Stitch

med yellow-green 4mm
Ribbon Stitch

dk gold 4mm
Twisted Ribbon Stitch

med dk red 7mm
Padded Straight Stitch
(Colonial Knot)

gold floss (1 strand)
Stem Stitch

green floss (1 strand)
Stem Stitch

dk gold 4mm
Ribbon Stitch

green floss (1 strand)
Stem Stitch

med dk red 7mm
Padded Straight Stitch
(Colonial Knot)

med gray-green 4mm
Straight Stitch

lt bright green 4mm
Padded Straight Stitch
(Straight Stitch)

dk red 4mm
Straight Stitch

For the pomegranate, use floss to Stem Stitch stems. Work Padded Straight Stitch (Straight Stitch over Colonial Knot) for fruit; top with three Straight Stitches. Work Padded Straight Stitch (Straight Stitch over Colonial Knot) topped with five Straight Stitches for flower. Add Ribbon Stitch leaves.

For olives, use floss to Stem Stitch stems; work fruit with Padded Straight Stitches (Straight Stitch over Straight Stitch) and leaves with Straight Stitches.

For barley, work same as wheat (above).

For grapes, use floss to Stem Stitch stems; work a cluster of Padded Straight Stitches (Straight Stitch over Colonial Knot) on a short stem and two leaf clusters with five Straight Stitches, making the middle one longer and on top.

For the center design, work two very short vertical Ribbon Stitches with an overlapping horizontal Straight Stitch. Work another short vertical Ribbon Stitch, overlapped with a longer horizontal Ribbon Stitch, then work two vertical Ribbon Stitches.

Hallah

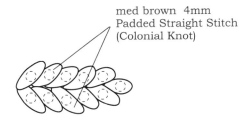

med brown 4mm
Padded Straight Stitch
(Colonial Knot)

Stitching order:
Working right to left, stitch two horizontal rows of Padded Straight Stitch (Straight Stitch over Colonial Knot), overlapping ends at center.

Pomegranate

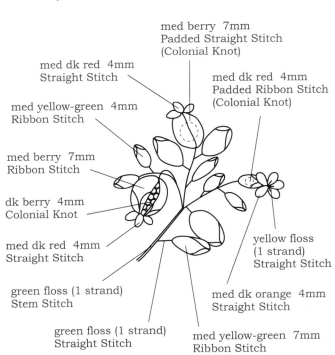

med berry 7mm
Padded Straight Stitch
(Colonial Knot)

med dk red 4mm
Straight Stitch

med dk red 4mm
Padded Ribbon Stitch
(Colonial Knot)

med yellow-green 4mm
Ribbon Stitch

med berry 7mm
Ribbon Stitch

dk berry 4mm
Colonial Knot

med dk red 4mm
Straight Stitch

yellow floss
(1 strand)
Straight Stitch

green floss (1 strand)
Stem Stitch

med dk orange 4mm
Straight Stitch

green floss (1 strand)
Straight Stitch

med yellow-green 7mm
Ribbon Stitch

Stitching order:
Use floss to Stem Stitch two parallel rows for the main stem, one row of Stem Stitch for remaining stems, and Straight Stitch the leaf stems. For the flower, work a Padded Ribbon Stitch (Ribbon Stitch over Colonial Knot) topped with five Straight Stitches plus floss Straight Stitches at center. For the top fruit, work Padded Straight Stitch (two Straight Stitches over a Colonial Knot); add three Straight Stitches at top. For the bottom (open) fruit, work an oval cluster of Colonial Knots. On the right side work a Ribbon Stitch, folding lengthwise in half before piercing. On the left side work a loose Ribbon Stitch. Add three Straight Stitches at end, and work Ribbon Stitch leaves.

Dreidl

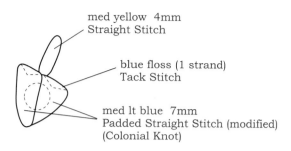

med yellow 4mm
Straight Stitch

blue floss (1 strand)
Tack Stitch

med lt blue 7mm
Padded Straight Stitch (modified)
(Colonial Knot)

Stitching order:
Work modified Padded Straight Stitch (two Straight Stitches over a Colonial Knot) and work a Straight Stitch for the handle.

Sukkah

Stitching order:
To make sukkah frame, work four vertical Straight Stitches for legs; add two horizontal and four diagonal Straight Stitches for top.

On right back leg, use floss to Stem Stitch stem; work myrtle with Ribbon Stitch leaves. At top, work a grape cluster of Colonial Knots topped with Ribbon Stitch leaves. For pear, work a Padded Straight Stitch (Straight Stitch over Colonial Knot), tacking near top to create shape; use floss to work Straight Stitches at bottom.

For the apple and the orange, work each with a Padded Straight Stitch (Straight Stitch over Colonial Knot) and a Ribbon Stitch for leaf. For the etrog fruit, work Padded Straight Stitch (two Straight Stitches over a French Knot). For palm on the back left leg, work a floss Wrapped Backstitch stem, topped with seven Straight Stitches. On the front left leg, use floss to work Stem Stitch stems; work Ribbon Stitches for willow leaves. For the vine, use floss to Stem Stitch stems; work Straight Stitches for leaves.

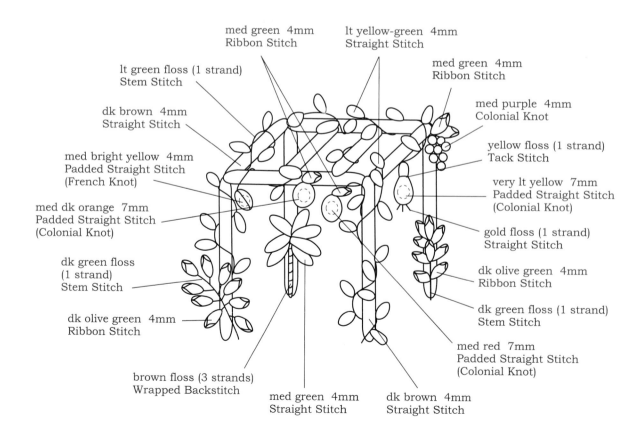

med green 4mm
Ribbon Stitch

lt yellow-green 4mm
Straight Stitch

lt green floss (1 strand)
Stem Stitch

med green 4mm
Ribbon Stitch

dk brown 4mm
Straight Stitch

med purple 4mm
Colonial Knot

med bright yellow 4mm
Padded Straight Stitch
(French Knot)

yellow floss (1 strand)
Tack Stitch

very lt yellow 7mm
Padded Straight Stitch
(Colonial Knot)

med dk orange 7mm
Padded Straight Stitch
(Colonial Knot)

gold floss (1 strand)
Straight Stitch

dk green floss
(1 strand)
Stem Stitch

dk olive green 4mm
Ribbon Stitch

dk green floss (1 strand)
Stem Stitch

dk olive green 4mm
Ribbon Stitch

med red 7mm
Padded Straight Stitch
(Colonial Knot)

brown floss (3 strands)
Wrapped Backstitch

med green 4mm
Straight Stitch

dk brown 4mm
Straight Stitch

50

Menorah

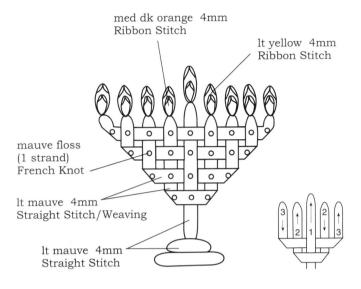

med dk orange 4mm
Ribbon Stitch

lt yellow 4mm
Ribbon Stitch

mauve floss
(1 strand)
French Knot

lt mauve 4mm
Straight Stitch/Weaving

lt mauve 4mm
Straight Stitch

Stitching order:
Begin at center with an upward vertical Straight Stitch (1) for main branch. At right and a bit lower, begin a downward Straight Stitch (2); three-fourths of the way down length of first stitch, fold ribbon diagonally, cross main branch, then fold again so ribbon is going upward, pinning in place. End stitch to match other side. Repeat for third stitch (3), starting at left of main branch and weaving under main branch. Work fourth and fifth stitches in same manner, randomly weaving and pinning while leaving a small space between stitches. Use floss to work French Knots over each intersection. Remove pins. For each flame, work a Ribbon Stitch, topped with a smaller Ribbon Stitch. For the base, work two overlapping horizontal Straight Stitches.

Star of David

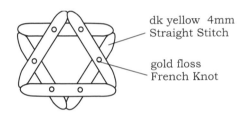

dk yellow 4mm
Straight Stitch

gold floss
French Knot

Stitching order:
Work three Straight Stitches in a triangle. Work an inverted second triangle on top; use floss to work French Knots at intersections.

Small Star of David

med brown 4mm
Straight Stitch/Weaving

Stitching order:
Work three Straight Stitches in a triangle; weave three Straight Stitches in an inverted triangle to form star.

Wheat

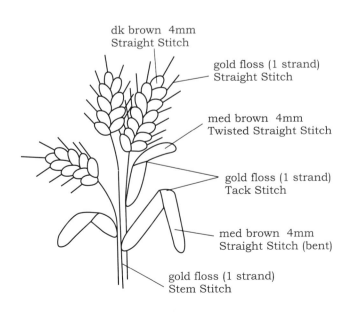

dk brown 4mm
Straight Stitch

gold floss (1 strand)
Straight Stitch

med brown 4mm
Twisted Straight Stitch

gold floss (1 strand)
Tack Stitch

med brown 4mm
Straight Stitch (bent)

gold floss (1 strand)
Stem Stitch

Stitching order:
Use floss to Stem Stitch stems; work one Twisted Straight Stitch leaf (tacking to retain shape) and two bent Straight Stitch leaves. To make a bent leaf, refer to "Bunny" on page 30. For the wheat, work two overlapping rows of Straight Stitches, beginning with a single stitch at the top. Use floss to work Straight Stitches at ends.

Thanksgiving

Mums

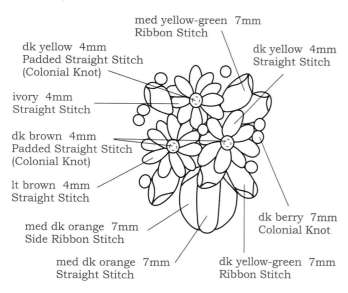

med yellow-green 7mm
Ribbon Stitch

dk yellow 4mm
Straight Stitch

dk yellow 4mm
Padded Straight Stitch
(Colonial Knot)

ivory 4mm
Straight Stitch

dk brown 4mm
Padded Straight Stitch
(Colonial Knot)

lt brown 4mm
Straight Stitch

med dk orange 7mm
Side Ribbon Stitch

med dk orange 7mm
Straight Stitch

dk berry 7mm
Colonial Knot

dk yellow-green 7mm
Ribbon Stitch

Stitching order:
For vase, work two Side Ribbon Stitches with a Straight Stitch centered on top. For leaves, work six Ribbon Stitches scattered above vase, with two lower ones overlapping vase. Between leaves, work Straight Stitch flowers with a Padded Straight Stitch (Straight Stitch over Colonial Knot) at each center. For berries, work Colonial Knots.

Fruit Pyramid

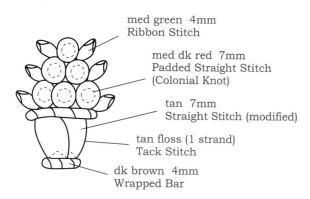

med green 4mm
Ribbon Stitch

med dk red 7mm
Padded Straight Stitch
(Colonial Knot)

tan 7mm
Straight Stitch (modified)

tan floss (1 strand)
Tack Stitch

dk brown 4mm
Wrapped Bar

Stitching order:
For urn, work two modified Straight Stitches, with Wrapped Bars for bottom and top rims. To make fruit, work a pyramid of Padded Straight Stitches (Straight Stitch over Colonial Knot), filling in with Ribbon Stitch leaves.

Bouquet of Autumn

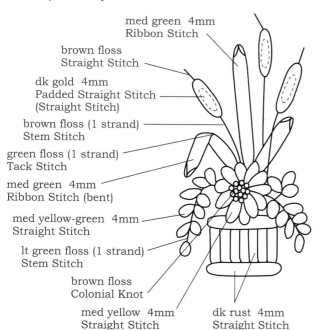

med green 4mm
Ribbon Stitch

brown floss
Straight Stitch

dk gold 4mm
Padded Straight Stitch
(Straight Stitch)

brown floss (1 strand)
Stem Stitch

green floss (1 strand)
Tack Stitch

med green 4mm
Ribbon Stitch (bent)

med yellow-green 4mm
Straight Stitch

lt green floss (1 strand)
Stem Stitch

brown floss
Colonial Knot

med yellow 4mm
Straight Stitch

dk rust 4mm
Straight Stitch

Stitching order:
For container, work vertical Straight Stitches, slightly overlapped at top and bottom with horizontal Straight Stitches. Work Straight Stitch flower petals and use floss to fill center with Colonial Knots. Use floss to work Stem Stitches curving downward from both sides of flower, and work Straight Stitch leaves alternately along stems. Above flower, work a long vertical Ribbon Stitch at center, a shorter one on right side, and a bent one on left side. To make a bent stitch, refer to "Bunny" on page 30. To make cattails, work floss Stem Stitches upward from flower; work Padded Straight Stitches (Straight Stitch over Straight Stitch), with floss Straight Stitch extensions.

Thanksgiving Wreath

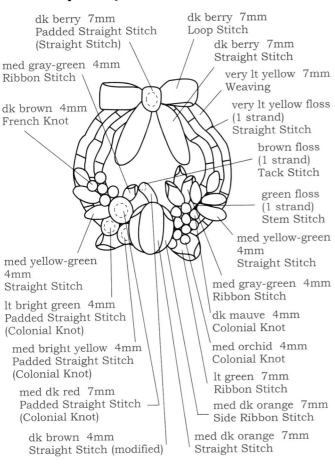

dk berry 7mm
Padded Straight Stitch
(Straight Stitch)

med gray-green 4mm
Ribbon Stitch

dk brown 4mm
French Knot

dk berry 7mm
Loop Stitch

dk berry 7mm
Straight Stitch

very lt yellow 7mm
Weaving

very lt yellow floss
(1 strand)
Straight Stitch

brown floss
(1 strand)
Tack Stitch

green floss
(1 strand)
Stem Stitch

med yellow-green
4mm
Straight Stitch

med yellow-green
4mm
Straight Stitch

lt bright green 4mm
Padded Straight Stitch
(Colonial Knot)

med bright yellow 4mm
Padded Straight Stitch
(Colonial Knot)

med dk red 7mm
Padded Straight Stitch
(Colonial Knot)

dk brown 4mm
Straight Stitch (modified)

med gray-green 4mm
Ribbon Stitch

dk mauve 4mm
Colonial Knot

med orchid 4mm
Colonial Knot

lt green 7mm
Ribbon Stitch

med dk orange 7mm
Side Ribbon Stitch

med dk orange 7mm
Straight Stitch

Stitching order:

A weaving technique is used for the wreath. For spokes to weave ribbon through, use floss to work Straight Stitches radiating outward in a large circle, leaving a gap at bottom. Beginning at one end, weave over and under the spokes to complete three rows. For bow, work two Loop Stitches with a Padded Straight Stitch (Straight Stitch over Straight Stitch) at center and two Straight Stitches for streamers. At bottom center of wreath, work a small pumpkin with a Straight Stitch centered over two Side Ribbon Stitches; top with a modified Straight Stitch stem.

To lower right of pumpkin, work one Ribbon Stitch leaf topped with a cluster of Colonial Knots in two colors. Work a floss Stem Stitch stem. Work Straight Stitch leaves along stem; work Ribbon Stitch leaves above grapes. To lower left of pumpkin, work one Ribbon Stitch leaf, topped with three Padded Straight Stitches (Straight Stitch over Colonial Knot). Add Ribbon Stitch and Straight Stitch leaves plus a cluster of French Knots.

Horn of Plenty

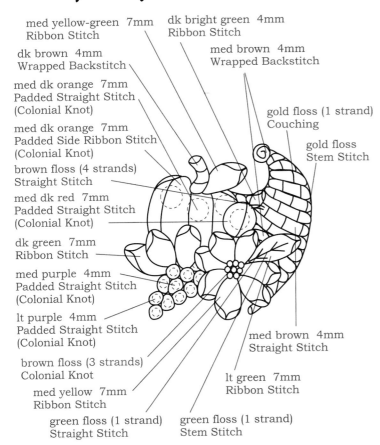

med yellow-green 7mm
Ribbon Stitch

dk brown 4mm
Wrapped Backstitch

med dk orange 7mm
Padded Straight Stitch
(Colonial Knot)

med dk orange 7mm
Padded Side Ribbon Stitch
(Colonial Knot)

brown floss (4 strands)
Straight Stitch

med dk red 7mm
Padded Straight Stitch
(Colonial Knot)

dk green 7mm
Ribbon Stitch

med purple 4mm
Padded Straight Stitch
(Colonial Knot)

lt purple 4mm
Padded Straight Stitch
(Colonial Knot)

brown floss (3 strands)
Colonial Knot

med yellow 7mm
Ribbon Stitch

green floss (1 strand)
Straight Stitch

dk bright green 4mm
Ribbon Stitch

med brown 4mm
Wrapped Backstitch

gold floss (1 strand)
Couching

gold floss
Stem Stitch

med brown 4mm
Straight Stitch

lt green 7mm
Ribbon Stitch

green floss (1 strand)
Stem Stitch

Stitching order:

For horn, use floss to Stem Stitch outer edge. Begin at tip and work parallel curved rows of Straight Stitches to fill space; Couch with floss. Work a circle of Wrapped Backstitch for tip and in a curve along front edge. For pumpkin, work two Padded Side Ribbon Stitches (Side Ribbon Stitch over Colonial Knot) topped with two Padded Straight Stitches (Straight Stitch over Colonial Knot) at center. Work a Wrapped Backstitch stem and Ribbon Stitch leaf. For grapes, work three Ribbon Stitch leaves and a cluster of Padded Straight Stitches (Straight Stitch over Colonial Knot) with two colors.

For apple, work Padded Straight Stitch (two Straight Stitches over a Colonial Knot) topped with a Ribbon Stitch leaf; use floss to Straight Stitch stem. For flower, work loose Ribbon Stitches in a circle; use floss to fill center with Colonial Knots. Next to flower, work a Ribbon Stitch leaf; use floss to Stem Stitch main vein and Straight Stitch side veins.

Christmas

Snowman

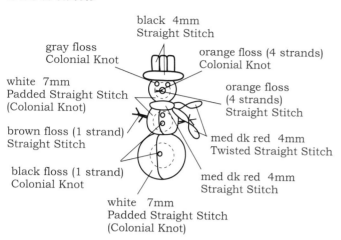

black 4mm
Straight Stitch

gray floss
Colonial Knot

orange floss (4 strands)
Colonial Knot

white 7mm
Padded Straight Stitch
(Colonial Knot)

orange floss
(4 strands)
Straight Stitch

brown floss (1 strand)
Straight Stitch

med dk red 4mm
Twisted Straight Stitch

black floss (1 strand)
Colonial Knot

med dk red 4mm
Straight Stitch

white 7mm
Padded Straight Stitch
(Colonial Knot)

Stitching order:
For head, work Padded Straight Stitch (Straight Stitch over Colonial Knot). Use floss to work Colonial Knot eyes and a Colonial Knot with a Straight Stitch for the nose. For each body section, work two Padded Straight Stitches (two Straight Stitches over a Colonial Knot). Use floss to work three Colonial Knot buttons and two Straight Stitch arms, tucking under sides of body. For scarf, work a horizontal Straight Stitch with two Twisted Straight Stitches for streamers. For hat, work three vertical Straight Stitches with a horizontal Straight Stitch overlapping top of head.

Christmas Tree Lights

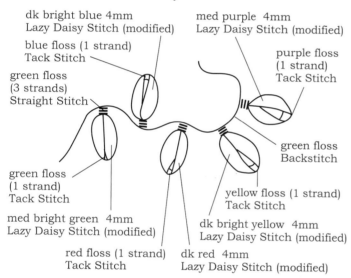

dk bright blue 4mm
Lazy Daisy Stitch (modified)

blue floss (1 strand)
Tack Stitch

green floss
(3 strands)
Straight Stitch

med purple 4mm
Lazy Daisy Stitch (modified)

purple floss
(1 strand)
Tack Stitch

green floss
Backstitch

green floss
(1 strand)
Tack Stitch

med bright green 4mm
Lazy Daisy Stitch (modified)

red floss (1 strand)
Tack Stitch

yellow floss (1 strand)
Tack Stitch

dk bright yellow 4mm
Lazy Daisy Stitch (modified)

dk red 4mm
Lazy Daisy Stitch (modified)

Stitching order:
Use floss to Backstitch cord. For each bulb, use floss to Straight Stitch the base, then work modified Lazy Daisies in desired colors, tacking to hold shape.

Ornaments

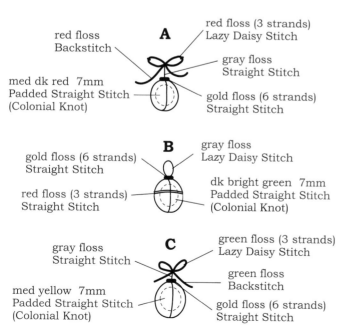

red floss
Backstitch

A

red floss (3 strands)
Lazy Daisy Stitch

gray floss
Straight Stitch

med dk red 7mm
Padded Straight Stitch
(Colonial Knot)

gold floss (6 strands)
Straight Stitch

gold floss (6 strands)
Straight Stitch

B

gray floss
Lazy Daisy Stitch

red floss (3 strands)
Straight Stitch

dk bright green 7mm
Padded Straight Stitch
(Colonial Knot)

gray floss
Straight Stitch

C

green floss (3 strands)
Lazy Daisy Stitch

green floss
Backstitch

med yellow 7mm
Padded Straight Stitch
(Colonial Knot)

gold floss (6 strands)
Straight Stitch

Stitching order:
Basic Ornament:
Work Padded Straight Stitch (two Straight Stitches over a loose Colonial Knot); to make a more rounded ball, begin and end Straight Stitch beneath center of padding knot.

Version A
Make basic ornament. Use floss to work horizontal Straight Stitches at top edge and a vertical Straight Stitch for hanger. For bow, use floss to work two Lazy Daisies and two Backstitch streamers.

Version B
Make basic ornament. Use floss to work horizontal Straight Stitches at top edge and and a Lazy Daisy for hook loop. On top of ornament, use floss to work a horizontal band of Straight Stitches.

Version C
Make ornament same as Version A.

St. Nicholas

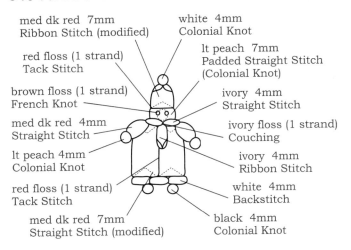

med dk red 7mm
Ribbon Stitch (modified)

red floss (1 strand)
Tack Stitch

brown floss (1 strand)
French Knot

med dk red 4mm
Straight Stitch

lt peach 4mm
Colonial Knot

red floss (1 strand)
Tack Stitch

med dk red 7mm
Straight Stitch (modified)

white 4mm
Colonial Knot

lt peach 7mm
Padded Straight Stitch
(Colonial Knot)

ivory 4mm
Straight Stitch

ivory floss (1 strand)
Couching

ivory 4mm
Ribbon Stitch

white 4mm
Backstitch

black 4mm
Colonial Knot

Stitching order:

For body, work two modified Straight Stitches, tacking to retain shape. For each arm, work a Straight Stitch with a Colonial Knot for hand. Work three Backstitches to trim bottom and two Colonial Knots for boots. For head, work a Padded Straight Stitch (Straight Stitch over Colonial Knot); use floss to work two French Knot eyes. Work a Ribbon Stitch for beard and a Straight Stitch couched at center for moustache. For hat, work a modified Ribbon Stitch, tacking to retain shape; top with a Colonial Knot.

Presents

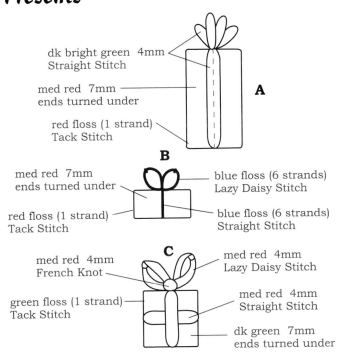

dk bright green 4mm
Straight Stitch

med red 7mm
ends turned under

red floss (1 strand)
Tack Stitch

A

B

med red 7mm
ends turned under

red floss (1 strand)
Tack Stitch

blue floss (6 strands)
Lazy Daisy Stitch

blue floss (6 strands)
Straight Stitch

C

med red 4mm
French Knot

green floss (1 strand)
Tack Stitch

med red 4mm
Lazy Daisy Stitch

med red 4mm
Straight Stitch

dk green 7mm
ends turned under

Stitching order:
Version A
Cut two pieces of ribbon. Place ribbons vertically parallel and pin ends under to create package shape; tack in place. Remove pins. For wrapping ribbon, work a vertical Straight Stitch; top with four Straight Stitches for bow.

Version B
Make package same as Version A. Use floss to Straight Stitch wrapping ribbon and make Lazy Daisy bow.

Version C
Make package same as Version A. For wrapping ribbon, work a horizontal Straight Stitch topped with a vertical Straight Stitch. For bow, work two Lazy Daisies with a French Knot at center.

Feather Tree

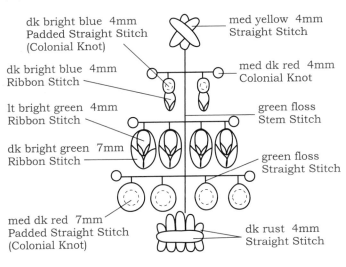

dk bright blue 4mm
Padded Straight Stitch
(Colonial Knot)

dk bright blue 4mm
Ribbon Stitch

lt bright green 4mm
Ribbon Stitch

dk bright green 7mm
Ribbon Stitch

med dk red 7mm
Padded Straight Stitch
(Colonial Knot)

med yellow 4mm
Straight Stitch

med dk red 4mm
Colonial Knot

green floss
Stem Stitch

green floss
Straight Stitch

dk rust 4mm
Straight Stitch

Stitching order:
For base of tree, work five vertical Straight Stitches, with the longest at center; work a horizontal Straight Stitch across middle. For tree trunk and branches, use floss to Stem Stitch one vertical row and three horizontal rows. Work Colonial Knots at ends of each horizontal row. Use floss to Straight Stitch all hanging stems. On the lowest row, work four Padded Straight Stitches (Straight Stitch over Colonial Knot). On the middle row work four Ribbon Stitches topped with four smaller Ribbon Stitches. On the top row work a Padded Straight Stitch (Straight Stitch over Colonial Knot) and a Ribbon Stitch for each ornament. At top of tree, work three Straight Stitches with the vertical one on the bottom.

Spruce Tree

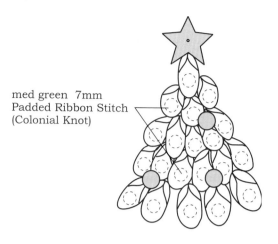

med green 7mm
Padded Ribbon Stitch
(Colonial Knot)

Trims:
Choose gold pebble beads (Mill Hill #0557) plus one 15mm gold star sequin and one gold seed bead.

Stitching order:
Work Padded Ribbon Stitches (Ribbon Stitch over Colonial Knot) in the shape of a triangle from bottom up, finishing with the last stitch centered at top. Using gold floss, sew pebble beads in tree; then sew star sequin held in place with seed bead at top.

Snowflakes

Stitching order:

Version A

A

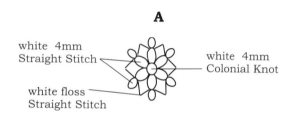

white 4mm
Straight Stitch

white 4mm
Colonial Knot

white floss
Straight Stitch

Work six Straight Stitches in a circle radiating from center with a Straight Stitch at each end; add a Colonial Knot at center. Use floss to work Straight Stitches forming peaks between Straight Stitch intersections.

Version B

B

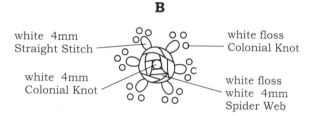

white 4mm
Straight Stitch

white floss
Colonial Knot

white 4mm
Colonial Knot

white floss
white 4mm
Spider Web

Use floss to work the base legs of a Spider Web; weave around spokes and work a Colonial Knot at center. Work six Straight Stitches radiating outward from Spider Web and three floss Colonial Knots at each end.

Version C

C

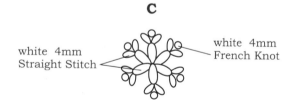

white 4mm
Straight Stitch

white 4mm
French Knot

Work six Straight Stitches in a circle radiating from center; work two Straight Stitches at each end with a French Knot at center.

Version D

D

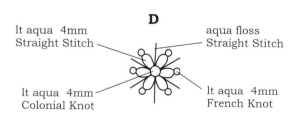

lt aqua 4mm
Straight Stitch

aqua floss
Straight Stitch

lt aqua 4mm
Colonial Knot

lt aqua 4mm
French Knot

Work six Straight Stitches in a circle radiating from center; adding a Colonial Knot at center. At the end of each Straight Stitch work a French Knot. Use floss to work radiating Straight Stitches between ribbon Straight Stitches.

Version E

E

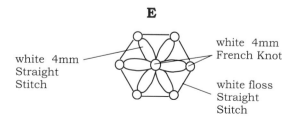

white 4mm
Straight
Stitch

white 4mm
French Knot

white floss
Straight
Stitch

Work six Straight Stitches in a circle radiating from center; add a French Knot at center. At the end of each Straight Stitch work a French Knot. Use floss to work Straight Stitches between outside knots.

Straw Wreath

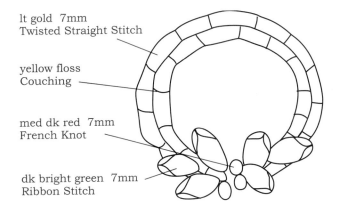

lt gold 7mm
Twisted Straight Stitch

yellow floss
Couching

med dk red 7mm
French Knot

dk bright green 7mm
Ribbon Stitch

Stitching order:
Cut a 7" piece of ribbon; bring ribbon up at center bottom and pin on fabric in a circular shape, occasionally twisting ribbon. Begin at one side and use floss to Couch at regular intervals to make a wreath shape; end off ribbon and remove pins. Repeat for inner circle. At bottom, work three French Knots with Ribbon Stitch leaves on each side.

Angel

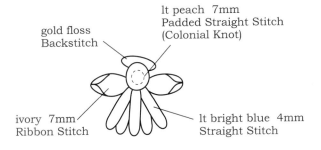

gold floss
Backstitch

lt peach 7mm
Padded Straight Stitch
(Colonial Knot)

ivory 7mm
Ribbon Stitch

lt bright blue 4mm
Straight Stitch

Stitching order:
For head, work a Padded Straight Stitch (Straight Stitch over Colonial Knot); use floss to Backstitch halo. For wings, work two Ribbon Stitches. For dress, work two Straight Stitches on each side with a Straight Stitch centered on top.

Candy Canes

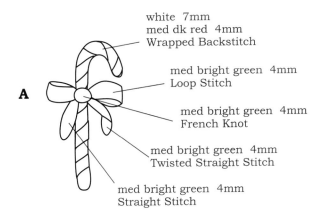

white 7mm
med dk red 4mm
Wrapped Backstitch

med bright green 4mm
Loop Stitch

med bright green 4mm
French Knot

med bright green 4mm
Twisted Straight Stitch

med bright green 4mm
Straight Stitch

A

Stitching order:
Version A
Work Wrapped Backstitch into a cane shape; work Backstitches with white and the slightly spaced wrapping with red. For bow, work two Loop Stitches with a French Knot at center, one Twisted Straight Stitch and one Straight Stitch for streamers.

Version B
Work Backstitches into a cane shape. Cover the joining points with Straight Stitches alternating with floss Straight Stitches.

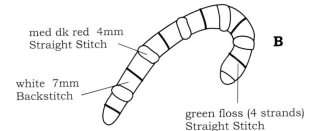

med dk red 4mm
Straight Stitch

white 7mm
Backstitch

B

green floss (4 strands)
Straight Stitch

Christmas Candy

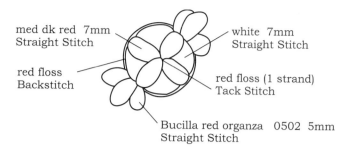

med dk red 7mm
Straight Stitch

white 7mm
Straight Stitch

red floss
Backstitch

red floss (1 strand)
Tack Stitch

Bucilla red organza 0502 5mm
Straight Stitch

Stitching order:
Work four radiating Straight Stitches and cover with two crossing Straight Stitches; use floss to tack at center and Backstitch around edges. At opposite ends, work three Straight Stitches with the longer center one on top.

Gingerbread Person

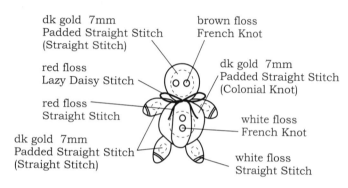

dk gold 7mm
Padded Straight Stitch
(Straight Stitch)

brown floss
French Knot

red floss
Lazy Daisy Stitch

dk gold 7mm
Padded Straight Stitch
(Colonial Knot)

red floss
Straight Stitch

white floss
French Knot

dk gold 7mm
Padded Straight Stitch
(Straight Stitch)

white floss
Straight Stitch

Stitching order:
For head, work Padded Straight Stitch (Straight Stitch over Straight Stitch). For body, work Padded Straight Stitch (three Straight Stitches over a Colonial Knot). Use floss to work French Knot eyes and buttons. For arms and legs, work Padded Straight Stitches (Straight Stitch over Straight Stitch); use floss to work Straight Stitches at ends. At neck, use floss to work two Lazy Daisies for bow and two Straight Stitches for streamers.

Plum Pudding

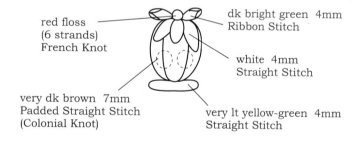

red floss
(6 strands)
French Knot

dk bright green 4mm
Ribbon Stitch

white 4mm
Straight Stitch

very dk brown 7mm
Padded Straight Stitch
(Colonial Knot)

very lt yellow-green 4mm
Straight Stitch

Stitching order:
Work three Padded Straight Stitches (Straight Stitch over two Colonial Knots); work three Straight Stitches on top with a floss French Knot at center and two Ribbon Stitches for leaves. For plate, work Straight Stitch.

Pomander

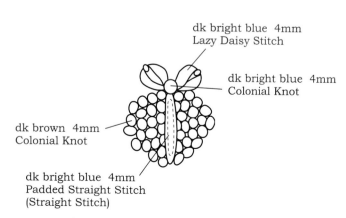

dk bright blue 4mm
Lazy Daisy Stitch

dk bright blue 4mm
Colonial Knot

dk brown 4mm
Colonial Knot

dk bright blue 4mm
Padded Straight Stitch
(Straight Stitch)

Stitching order:
Work a vertical Padded Straight Stitch (Straight Stitch over Straight Stitch); at top center, work two Lazy Daisies and a Colonial Knot. On each side of vertical ribbon, work a half circle of closely spaced Colonial Knots.

Star

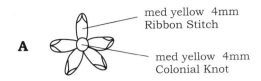

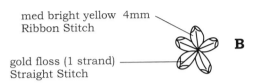

A med yellow 4mm
Ribbon Stitch

med yellow 4mm
Colonial Knot

med bright yellow 4mm
Ribbon Stitch

B

gold floss (1 strand)
Straight Stitch

Stitching order:

Version A

Work five Ribbon Stitches in shape of a star, and add a Colonial Knot at center.

Version B

Work five Ribbon Stitches in shape of a star, and use floss to top each stitch with a Straight Stitch.

Poinsettia

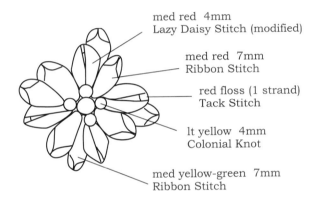

med red 4mm
Lazy Daisy Stitch (modified)

med red 7mm
Ribbon Stitch

red floss (1 strand)
Tack Stitch

lt yellow 4mm
Colonial Knot

med yellow-green 7mm
Ribbon Stitch

Stitching order:

Work four modified Lazy Daisies, alternately with four Ribbon Stitches in a circle; fill the center with one large and four smaller Colonial Knots. For leaves, work Ribbon Stitches, beginning each beneath a petal.

Mistletoe

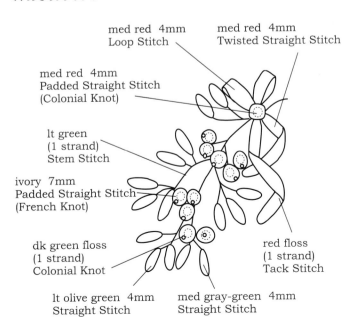

med red 4mm
Loop Stitch

med red 4mm
Twisted Straight Stitch

med red 4mm
Padded Straight Stitch
(Colonial Knot)

lt green
(1 strand)
Stem Stitch

ivory 7mm
Padded Straight Stitch
(French Knot)

dk green floss
(1 strand)
Colonial Knot

red floss
(1 strand)
Tack Stitch

lt olive green 4mm
Straight Stitch

med gray-green 4mm
Straight Stitch

Stitching order:

Starting at top, use floss to Stem Stitch stems. At the end of each short stem, work two or three Padded Straight Stitches (Straight Stitch over French Knot), topped with a Colonial Knot for berries. Work leaves in Straight Stitches. For bow, work two Loop Stitches, with a Padded Straight Stitch (Straight Stitch over Colonial Knot) at center. Work two Twisted Straight Stitches for streamers, tacking where needed to hold shape.

Cranberry 'n Popcorn Garland

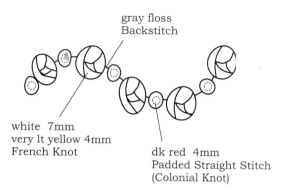

gray floss
Backstitch

white 7mm
very lt yellow 4mm
French Knot

dk red 4mm
Padded Straight Stitch
(Colonial Knot)

Stitching order:
Use floss to Backstitch string. For popcorn, work loose French Knots with two ribbons in needle, wrapping twice. For cranberries, work Padded Straight Stitch (Straight Stitch over Colonial Knot) alternately with popcorn.

Christmas Rose

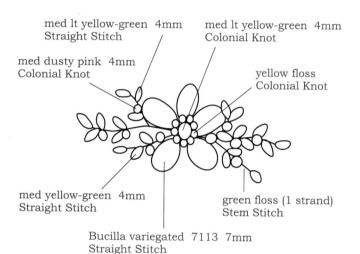

med lt yellow-green 4mm
Straight Stitch

med lt yellow-green 4mm
Colonial Knot

med dusty pink 4mm
Colonial Knot

yellow floss
Colonial Knot

med yellow-green 4mm
Straight Stitch

green floss (1 strand)
Stem Stitch

Bucilla variegated 7113 7mm
Straight Stitch

Note: This rose may be worked in either variegated white-to-pink ribbon or any desired pale pink ribbon.

Stitching order:
Work five loose Straight Stitches in a circle; at center work one large Colonial Knot surrounded with small floss Colonial Knots. On each side of flower, use floss to Stem Stitch stems. Add Straight Stitch leaves and Colonial Knot berries.

Noel

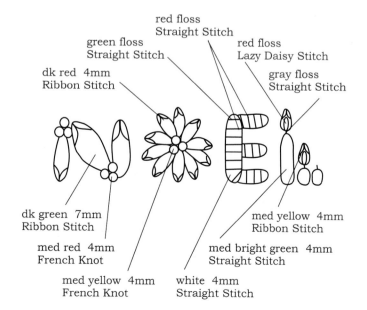

red floss
Straight Stitch

green floss
Straight Stitch

red floss
Lazy Daisy Stitch

dk red 4mm
Ribbon Stitch

gray floss
Straight Stitch

dk green 7mm
Ribbon Stitch

med yellow 4mm
Ribbon Stitch

med red 4mm
French Knot

med bright green 4mm
Straight Stitch

med yellow 4mm
French Knot

white 4mm
Straight Stitch

Stitching order:
To make "N," work three Ribbon Stitches with three French Knots at each joint. For the "O," work Ribbon Stitches in a circle with three French Knots at center. For the "E," work four Straight Stitches; use floss to work Straight Stitch stripes. For the "L," work three Straight Stitches. Use floss to Straight Stitch wicks. To each of the first two, add a Ribbon Stitch topped with a floss Lazy Daisy for flame.

60